KU-406-160

STEWART COWLEY

# The Golden Homes Book of
# PLANTS FOR POTS

**Golden Hands Books**

Marshall Cavendish
London and New York

Edited by Ursula Robertshaw and Lynn Dicknett

Published by Marshall Cavendish Publications Limited,
58 Old Compton Street, London W1V 5PA

© Marshall Cavendish Limited, 1968, 1970, 1973, 1975

Some of this material has previously appeared in
the partworks Encyclopedia of Gardening and Golden Homes and
in the publication Flowers and Plants in the Home.

First printing 1973.
Second printing 1975.
ISBN 0 85685 031 4.

Printed in Belgium by Henri Proost.

This edition is not to be sold in the United States,
Canada or the Philippines.

# Introduction

One of the great frustrations of life for city dwellers today is having to exist far away from the countryside. For many, the only living outlet available is a plant in the house, on the office window-sill, in window boxes or on tiny patios.

But even a few plants can help to satisfy the old Adam the Gardener in all of us for they will give months of pleasure while flowers are dead within a few days. And in our cramped cities, with their functional architecture, plants are a sign of natural life and individuality that is more than welcome.

No matter how much space you have available, no matter where that space is, then this is the book for you. It tells you which plants to grow on a window-ledge, in the office, on a balcony, in your living-room, around a patio and anywhere else that you can find the space for a pot or tub.

It tells you how to feed, water and care for your plants, how to make sure they stay as healthy as you do, and how to get the most out of them by careful design of the space you have available. Every question you are ever likely to ask about house plants – those that can spend their whole time indoors – and pot plants – those that you can bring indoors for a while – you will find answered here.

Whether you choose a Sanseviera, which is almost unkillable, or a Saintpaulia, which needs continual care, *Plants for Pots* will tell you where to keep it, how to look after it and how to display it at its best. With this book at your side growing plants will be more than a hobby – it will become a lasting pleasure.

The jungly plants: Begonia Rex (Fan Plant) (left), Monstera Deliciosa (Swiss Cheese or Mexican Breadfruit) (centre), Philodendron Scandens (Sweetheart Plant) (right).

# Contents

# How plants can enliven your home

## Creating gardens out of nothing

Many people who live in town flats or houses without gardens are resigned to having no natural colour or foliage around their house. But even if you have no grass or flower beds, it is possible to create the illusion of a garden, using a lot of imagination and a little money.

The awkward-shaped areas behind terrace houses are often crazy paved, leaving no beds or lawns round which to plan a conventional garden. However, a 'man-made' garden can be easier to manage, and avoids the necessity of mowing patches of grass and weeding borders.

Painting the back of the house white up to the first-floor level cheers up a dark yard and reflects all the available light. Window boxes can add splashes of colour high up.

Climbing or trailing plants can camouflage ugly sheds or dustbins, or separate your property from a neighbour's. Rambling Roses look attractive clinging to a wall or against the house. Trees in tubs outside your front door smarten up the entrance of the house.

A climbing plant can easily be put in the corner of a concreted yard and encouraged to climb up the house. Plants pushed at random into the holes between paving slabs or bricks in a yard or path create an informal effect.

Hanging baskets, wheelbarrows, kettles, Provençal earthenware pots, terracotta strawberry pots, even chamber pots – the list of possible containers for plants is endless. But they don't have to be elaborate to look good. Even a row of ordinary earthenware flower pots can have a stunning effect lined up at the foot of a wall or on a window sill.

Most people think of a garden as being at ground level, but many town dwellers find that their roofs and even balconies can easily be transformed into colourful areas.

A roof garden can be an imaginatively-designed sitting-out place covered with all kinds of attractive plants and flowers – the days of the tatty corner, sparingly set with a few straggly pot plants, are over.

A roof garden can be a jungle of exotic, creeping and trailing plants, sculptures, earthenware jugs and coloured lights for evening illumination.

Wicker chairs and occasional tables arranged on the tinted cement floor can give the whole area a real country atmosphere. The same ideas could be used by anyone with a town house to lessen the usual feeling of having nothing to look at but brickwork.

## Balconies

For town-dwellers a balcony, if you are lucky enough to have one, offers an opportunity to create a miniature garden. Like window boxes and hanging baskets a balcony can improve the dreariest outlook. It is so much nicer to look at green growing things and colourful groups of flowers than to be forced to stare at the windows of the house opposite.

Even on the smallest balcony (or flat roof) it is possible to use the space to grow decorative plants, and even useful plants like one or two pots of Tomatoes, or a big pot of Green Beans climbing up canes. If space is very limited, and the position is sheltered enough for them, make use of the wall by having climbing plants.

Some good annual climbers are *Cobaea Scandens* (the Cup and Saucer plant) which has greenish-white flowers changing to violet as the flowers mature, and can cover a wall in a summer as it grows up to 10 feet high up strings or a lattice; *Rudbeckia Hirta* (Black-eyed Susan) which does best in semi-shade and is covered in vivid yellow flowers from mid-summer until autumn.

The most beautiful of all the annual climbers are, perhaps, the *Ipomoea* (Heavenly Blue or Morning Glory) which lives up to its name with its brilliant shining blue trumpets, climbs up canes or string and does best in a sheltered place with a great deal of sun, and *Passiflora Caerulea* (Passion Flower) which is equally delicate and has beautiful sculptural flowers. For a narrow little box or sink garden in a less sheltered spot *Sempervivums* (House Leeks) are lovely. They spread and propagate themselves and are as tough as you could wish. Other alpine-type plants, such as some of the *Saxifrages*, could be planted with them.

On a shady balcony you could grow *Begonias*, *Fuchsias*, Ferns, and trailing Vines, in pots and tubs. For a sunnier spot *Petunias* will be happier.

In window boxes use winter evergreens like small Junipers and Cypresses, and tough little Heathers and Ivies. Either move these into the garden in spring, or put your flowers among them.

## Hanging baskets

A basket can look extremely attractive hanging in a porch, on a balcony, or under a verandah. Like window boxes and pot plants, they are a way of compensating for the lack of a garden, so do try to put them where you will enjoy them from indoors – not where they are only visible from outside the house.

You can have hanging baskets indoors, but line them with green plastic or buy special watertight baskets which have their own interior draining devices – otherwise you will have drips all over the floor each time you water.

### Size, soil and succour
The basket itself should be at least 9 inches in diameter; if it is smaller than this it will not really hold enough soil to keep many types of plant healthy. Ideally it should be 1-1½ feet in diameter and have a depth of 6-9 inches.

Hanging baskets are planted at the beginning of summer, to be hung up outside when all danger of frost is past. Make sure you hang them from a strong support, as they can get very heavy. Line them with moss, this will help to retain as much water as possible, and then fill them with a mixture of peat and potting soil. They must not be allowed to dry out and in the driest weather must be watered twice a day. If possible, it is better occasionally to take the basket down and immerse it in water rather than water it overhead. If you have very leafy plants, *Zebrinas* for example, clean their leaves occasionally by spraying or wiping them.

### Where to hang them
Site the baskets carefully so that they do not cut out any light from the house. They must also be easy to water, but not so low that they thump unwary heads and not where they may drip on the innocent caller.

### Which plants to choose
Plants which trail naturally are best: Ivies, *Lobelias*, pendant *Begonias*, *Petunias*, *Zebrinas*, *Chlorophytum* (Spider Plant) and *Pelargoniums* (particularly the ivy-leaved varieties), with Nasturtiums sown among them to roar away at the end of the summer. Trailing *Fuchsias* can look lovely, too, but they need plenty of space in which to grow and dislike draughts.

## Small conservatories

An attractive and unusual idea is to put shelves across a bay window and have a mixed group of flowering and foliage plants. Outside you could have a window box so that the whole window is a mass of growing things. (Not, of course, if it is a darkish room or a room in which people have to work.) A hall or landing window is ideal for this.

On the shelves grow pots of Ferns, Geraniums, *Tradescantia*, *Begonias*, *Hoyas*, *Solanum*, and trailing Ivies are particularly attractive.

Alternatively, if your house has a verandah you could have this glassed in and turned into a small conservatory, giving yourself an extension to the house – a garden room.

If this room receives a lot of sun you could grow Cacti and other desert plants. If it is warm but shady, receiving little direct sun, create a jungle atmosphere. Grow *Begonias*, *Philodendrons*, *Monsteras*, and some of the tropical Ferns. Keep the humidity up by hosing down a stone floor each day and leaving it to steam-dry.

# Two tiny gardens

This yard (left) has been transformed by a variety of plants in pots and tubs. A trellis fixed to the top of the dividing brick wall gives a neighbour's Russian vine something to trail along, while the standard foliage gives colourful interest at medium height. Lower down, two large wooden tubs are brimming over with begonias and pelargoniums.

Any marble object adds a rich touch to a garden, and here a white marble buttress has been fixed against the wall of the house. The scene is completed by two artificial stone lions outside the door guarding the house.

An idea with an area such as this is to remove some of the paving slabs, put a thick layer of earth in the holes, and plant bulbs in them. Tulips or small conifers look good in formal settings such as this, and do not hang over the paths and get in the way.

Conifers are available in a wide range of shapes and colours, and you can buy some special dwarfed species that will never grow too big. They are all evergreen, and give colour all the year round. There are green, blue, grey, yellow and bronze conifers, which can be chosen to tone with the other shrubs and plants in your garden.

The photograph on the left shows a formal arrangement in a courtyard which has been covered in square concrete paving slabs.

In the foreground, a weeping cherry tree in a simulated lead tub gracefully frames the area, with pelargoniums at its base. A dwarf conifer fills the square tub on the right of the door. Outside the window are low clumps of pelargoniums and African marigolds in an attractive collection of terracotta troughs and pots. They not only add colour at ground level, but are also visible from inside the house.

This first-floor garden (left) has been created outside a large living room on the flat roof of the kitchen extension below. The living-room window has been replaced by French doors, so that the roof garden now merges with it. In this way, a feeling of openness is created, in spite of the lack of a conventional garden.

In winter, the area is enclosed in clear acrylic panels which let in daylight but keep out the weather. These panels are removed in summer, when the intercommunicating French doors can be left open to link the house with the roof garden.

1 A formally arranged courtyard which has been paved over with concrete slabs.
2 A first-floor garden cleverly arranged on top of a kitchen extension below.

## Basements

The area outside the window of a basement room can be filled with plants, and the walls painted white to reflect light. The greenery is flattered by its white surroundings, giving a fresh, summery look to the 'garden' above.

Plants in low tubs can be set around the walls inside the room (above a *Rhoicissus rhomboidea* in a flower pot echoes the jungle theme) to extend the 'garden' into the house. Concealed lighting completes the effect.

No space has been wasted in this basement garden room. Pivoting glazed doors reaching right up to street level provide access to the two vaults under the pavement, which give a fascinating catacomb effect.

The white-painted brick walls not only tighten the area, but also give an illusion of more space. White stone chippings cover the floor.

## Flower troughs

Flower troughs and tubs of any shape and size can quite easily be cast in concrete, and either left in their natural state or painted. Filled with a peat-based compost (to avoid too much weight) and planted with a colourful selection of flowers they are a bright addition to any dull back yard or path.

An ordinary glazed fireclay kitchen sink can be made into an attractive plant trough by the application of a mixture which the Royal Horticultural Society of Great Britain calls Hypatufa.

It consists of 1 part cement, 1 part sharp sand, and 2 parts dry sifted sphagnum peat (measured by bulk, not weight). These are mixed together with water to a firm paste that can be applied to a vertical surface without sliding off.

Make sure the sink is absolutely clean, and free from grease. Paint the outside surface with a concrete bonding agent such as Unibond and when this is nearly dry, but still tacky, apply a coat of Hypatufa about $\frac{1}{4}$ inch thick.

The dampness of the trough's contents will soon make it develop a mossy appearance, and plants will cling to it and completely disguise its shape.

**1** Making the best of the usually dull area outside a basement.
**2** Using a simple concrete container can make any patio or garden look much more attractive with planted flowers.

## Handling plants correctly

Pot plants are not just decorative objects that fill up the odd corner of a room which would otherwise look bare; handled correctly they can be an integral part of interior design and add enormously to the total look of your home. There is a vast range to choose from, including flowering and shrub-like plants, and those noted for their shape and colour of their foliage. Looked after carefully they can last for years, and if arranged with thought and imagination, groups of plants can look like living sculptures.

## Healthy plants look best

Plants can only look their best if they are healthy. Tall, leafless plants, yellowing and bedraggled leaves or rock-hard compost are sure signs that a plant has a short, unglamourous future. Choose plants from a reputable shop or nursery and be careful to protect them from the weather on the journey to your house. A stout polythene bag secured over the plant will keep extremes of temperature from affecting the blooms or delicate leaves.

Pot plants tend to live happily in groups – one plant in splendid isolation not only looks lost, but often dies prematurely. But when selecting plants for grouping, make sure that they need roughly the same amount of water and nourishment, and thrive in the same conditions. For example it is unwise to mix plants that need a cool dry atmosphere with plants that can only live in moist warm conditions. And some need light to keep them healthy while others can flourish in several degrees of shade. It is always a good idea to do your homework, and ask a good florist or nurseryman about the most promising conditions for your indoor garden.

## Temperature and humidity

The amount of warmth a plant needs depends, naturally enough, upon what its native conditions were like. Sub-tropical plants need more warmth than the hardy northern species. Generally speaking, the temperature in your living room in winter dictates the choice of house plants.

The one thing to remember here is that few plants can survive extreme changes in temperature. So, if a plant lives on a windowsill, then in winter you must move it into the room at night – proximity to cold glass could give it frost-bite.

A further complication, which is becoming more of a problem as houses get hotter and hotter, is the temperature preferred by humans living in the house. If they decide to raise the temperature to 21°C (70°F) then even plants which like a hot temperature will object because of a lack of humidity – that is, moisture in the air. As far as plants are concerned, the higher the temperature the greater the humidity should be. But unfortunately this usually does not follow; modern heating methods all tend to dry the air.

You must, therefore, create a humid atmosphere for your plants. Either spray them, or put pebbles in the saucers on which you stand your pots, and pour water in the saucer – making sure it does not cover the pebbles. As the water evaporates it will give a humid atmosphere around the plants.

## Watering

It is difficult to be dogmatic about watering. Every plant has individual needs depending upon its situation, the time of year, and what sort of plant it is.

The only general rule to follow is never to allow the soil to become completely dry. You can test the soil by touch; other indications are that dry soil is lighter both in colour and weight.

If it is very dry, plunge the pot into a bucket of water and leave it until air bubbles stop coming to the surface. This must not be done to plants such as Cyclamens and African Violets where water on the corm could be fatal.

Water plants thoroughly, not in drips. Fill the space between the soil and the rim of the pot with water, wait about 30 minutes, and then throw away any water which has collected in the saucer below the pot. Never leave a plant standing with its feet in water.

In the dormant winter season plants need comparatively little water, while in spring and summer when they are making new growth they are extremely thirsty. Rain water is best for indoor plants, as for any plants. But if this is not available, tap water which has stood at room temperature for a few hours is satisfactory.

Most plants appreciate a spray from time to time – you could use an old perfume atomizer for this – and those with large, fleshy, shiny leaves should be sponged gently to rid them of any dust.

## Watering during holidays

When you go away on holiday plants can pose almost as big a problem as pets. Winter holidays are quite easy to cater for. Move the plants away from windows, grouping them together in the centre of the room. Water them so that the soil is well-moistened, then surround each pot with damp peat to give extra, longer-lasting moisture.

Summer holidays do create difficulties because at this time plants are growing and in need of regular feeding and watering. The best idea really is to persuade a friend to call in occasionally and look after your plants. If, however, this is not possible then trim off any flower buds, move the plants to the centre of a room out of the sun, water them thoroughly, surround the pots with damp peat and, finally, cover the soil with sodden newspaper. Alternatively, some of the hardier plants could be planted in their pots in a shady corner of the garden. Or you could buy a self-watering device from a florist.

## Feeding

You can tell when a plant needs food simply by looking at it – if the leaves look small and growth has slowed down it is undernourished. This happens to pot plants because they are limited to a small amount of soil, whereas garden plants can send their roots out over a larger area in search of food.

Feeding should not be necessary for a year after the plant has been bought or re-potted, and then only when the plant is making new growth. Some plant foods are liquid; some are powders; all come with directions which must be followed. Feed at regular intervals. Overfeeding will do no good as the plant can only use so much, and it could in some cases be as lethal as over-watering.

## Grouping your plants

A large plant standing alone will look very attractive but it is also a good idea to group plants together, rather than dot them around a room.

### Plant troughs
Plant trays or troughs (available from gardening shops) can look very effective. Stand the pots on a bed of gravel or pebbles in the bottom of the trough and pack peat or moss between them. (You can put about the top some of your favourite holiday-gathered sea pebbles which will help to stop evaporation.) The plants are then all watered together, the moisture rises through the gravel surrounding the plants. (In this way, they need watering less.)

You could choose plants for the trough for the contrast of their foliage; glossy, shiny green, feathery, sculptural and stiff, or trailing and delicate. Of course you must be sure that all members of your group like the same conditions. If a plant unfortunately dies, simply remove its pot and replace it with another plant.

Large picture windows can have a plant trough running along their length. And another ideal spot for a plant trough, if there is enough light, is a disused fireplace – with the chimney blocked off, of course, to cut out damaging draughts. By grouping your plants and by caring for them well you can improve your surroundings immeasurably.

Colourful plants grouped in a deep kitchen window can be used to shut out a dismal view (above). A hanging basket full of gay flowers adds to the rural charm of this house (below).

Hanging baskets, creeping plants and plants with sculptural shapes have been used in this small Victorian conservatory and combine to give it an authentic period atmosphere (right).

## Window boxes

Window boxes serve two functions; the first is to decorate the outside of a house, thus giving pleasure not only to the owner but also to passers-by, and the second is to add to the pleasure of those inside by giving them a tiny foreground landscape of flower and leaf through, or across, which to look at the world. The view through a window is much improved on a grey morning if it is seen past the nodding heads of Daffodils or Pot Marigolds.

### How many boxes
The shape, size and number of window boxes will, obviously, be dictated by the house itself. If you have just one window box it should be colourful and well-tended – it must merit the attention it will undoubtedly receive. Alternatively, you could have a mixture of troughs, pots and window boxes – each filled with different varieties of flower. Just think of those pavements, yards, and flights of steps in the Mediterranean countries where every kind of pot and pan, even painted petrol tins, contains a glittering cascade of bright flowers which enliven the dullest corner.

### Making a window box
Even if you cannot find a space in your house where you can make a garden out of nothing, you are bound to have a window sill, either inside or out. Here, a box filled with pretty flowers can be a colourful alternative to no garden at all.

A well-stocked and well-tended window box can make up for the lack of a garden. It becomes a feature for both you and your neighbours to enjoy, and enhances the look of a house by softening harsh outlines and brightening expanses of dull masonry. This cheerful addition to your home can be made very simply.

The best wood to use is prepared softwood 10 in. x 1 in. or 12 in. x 1 in. (250 mm x 25 mm or 300 mm x 25 mm). Either of these widths makes a good height for the box, allowing room for plenty of drainage material under the soil, and at the same time giving the roots of the plants sufficient airing. The length and width of the box should be calculated according to the size of the window sill, or the available space.

The diagram shows the front and back pieces, the sides and the base. To make a good-looking job of the window box, make sure you fit the sides and the base *inside* the front and the back so that the end grain of the wood used to make the sides and base does not show in front.

Drill two rows of ½ in. (13 mm) diameter holes for drainage at 4-5 in. (100-125 mm) intervals in the base. Glue and screw the pieces together, using brass screws and a waterproof glue such as a urea formaldehyde type.

Finish the top of the box with a capping of ¾ in. (19 mm) half-round moulding or flat strips of hardwood. This is the only difficult part of the construction, because the ends have to be mitred. Pin and glue the moulding to the box.

If the box is going to be placed on a window sill, it is wise to stand it on two battens to enable excess water to drain away. These should be 1 in. (25 mm)

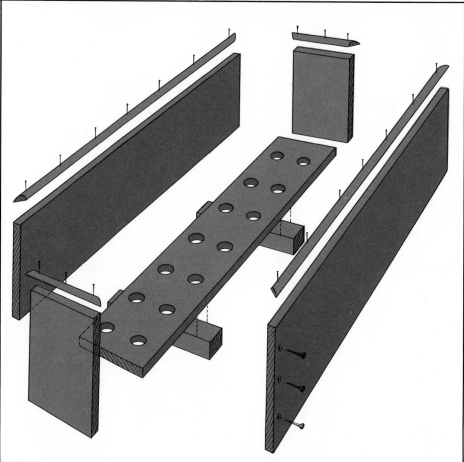

1 An old kitchen sink makes a delightful window box.
2 Making a wooden window-box is not a difficult task.
3 The best use of a tiny space.

longer than the width of the box, and screwed on to its base. They will not be needed, however, if the box is mounted on brackets screwed to the wall. You can use the metal brackets sold by ironmongers, or make them yourself from wood.

Do not forget to secure the window box in position, whether it is placed on a window sill or fitted against a wall. Fix a screw-eye on each side, and hooks on the wall or window frame, to hold the box firmly in bad weather.

Once the assembly is completed, the next step is to paint the inside thoroughly with a 'horticultural grade' wood preservative which is harmless to plants. Allow this to dry for at least 10 hours and apply a second coat. Leave it to dry as before, then apply the third and final coat. If you want a natural-wood effect, treat the outside with clear polyurethane varnish. If you want to paint the box, use an exterior grade paint.

Now the box is ready to be filled. First cover the drainage holes with pieces of broken earthenware flower pots, followed by a layer of gravel or crocks to a depth of 1½ in. (40 mm). This provides good drainage, and prevents the soil from getting stale or sour.

Next comes the soil, which can make a large box very heavy. A peat-based mixture is suitable and relatively light, but a compost soil such as John Innes No. 2 is better if the volume needed doesn't make the box too heavy. Fill the box up to 1 in. (25 mm) from the top.

If a filling of soil would make the window box too heavy, or it would be difficult to work at when in position, it is a good idea to put your plants in pots and arrange them on a shallow tray placed in the bottom of the box. The pots can then easily be lifted out when you want to tend or replace them, without leaning out of the window.

Short, small plants look very smart and are also much easier to manage when keeping a box in good trim. It is advisable to avoid large plants, as they will very soon give the box an untidy and overgrown appearance. Certain plants require deeper soil than 12 in. for root travel, so if you are in doubt you should ask someone at your gardening centre for advice.

### A window box of herbs
Sweet-smelling Rosemary and Lavender are good window box plants, and if you have a convenient sill and are devoted to cooking have a box for more of your favourite herbs. Many useful ones – Chives, Chervil, Parsley, Savory, Thyme and Marjoram – will thrive in a box if they are kept well-watered.

A hanging basket is an effective way of providing your home with flowers and foliage at an extra level. Generally they are made of wire and suspended by chains from the ceiling or the porch at the front of the house. Fill them with brightly coloured plants, or Ivies that trail over the side of the basket adding interesting lines to the arrangement. Usually the excess water simply drains through the bottom of the basket so make sure that it doesn't hang directly over furniture or carpets. Hanging baskets look good against whitewashed walls and brickwork.

A plant window is simply a trough filled with various flowering and leafy plants, taking the place of the usual window sill and using the whole width of the window. Choose plants that differ widely in shape and height, but make sure that they need the same amount of sunlight and roughly the same amount of water. The outline of the leaves and blooms will be silhouetted dramatically against the window at dusk and in the early morning.

A plant trough is similar to a plant window, but here the plants stay in their individual pots and therefore they can have different cultural requirements. The trough should hide the top of all the pots and should be watertight. It can be made of almost any material though the most effective are generally of natural materials such as wood or carved stone.

*Jardinieres* are troughs or large pots which are decorative objects in their own right. The individual pots can be swapped round so that the overall look of the arrangement is varied.

A single pot need not be boring. Bushy plants such as the popular 'Spider Plant' will always look effective on their own, as will healthy flowering plants such as Azaleas. Types with small leaves look best grouped together on a table, otherwise small plants by themselves tend to look 'lost'. Keep them away from draughts or blasts of hot air from heaters.

A log or bark centrepiece is an unusual and eyecatching creation using the natural texture of the bark to set off your plants which would grow on bark in nature. Take the plant out of its pot and wrap the roots in moist sphagnum moss and secure it to the bark. When the roots grow the plant will become firmly attached to the bark.

A miniature garden is usually a scaled-down representation of a real Japanese garden, including tree-like plants, streams, paths and even miniature figures. These 'gardens' are displayed in shallow bowls rather like indoor gardens. Bottle gardens are impressive but simple creations which go well with modern interiors. They are made by planting slow-growing and smallish plants in the bottom of a large carboy and watering with a narrow-spouted can.

A wall bracket display saves space on sideboards and tables, and provides interest on what may otherwise be a boring wall. Ivies and flowering plants are usual for these displays and can draw attention to a particularly favourite picture or wall ornament by framing it or highlighting it, thus carrying the eye in that direction. Pale, otherwise featureless walls benefit greatly from wall displays which give them a focal point and 'life'. Make sure that the bracket is secure and that each plant is stood in a sufficiently deep saucer.

An indoor garden is a fine focus for any room. It is a group of house plants growing together in one container. Ideally each arrangement should have at least one plant trailing down over the edge of the bowl and one to carry the eye upwards as contrast. Use plants with different leaf colours for a more attractive display.

Climbing displays are especially effective in large rooms or offices where they can be used as room dividers, or to frame large windows. If you want to block out the view altogether use densely leaved climbers, or if you want merely a decorative effect then some of the fast-growing Ivies would be suitable, especially with two-tone leaves.

Pot-et-fleur displays are artistic ways of creating mixed arrangements of house plants and fresh flowers in the same container. Tubes are embedded in the soil, filled with water, and then the flowers are arranged in them. Naturally the flowers will have to be replaced in a short time, but the plants which surround them form a more permanent background. Draw attention to the flowers by using only leafy plants.

17

Almost anything – provided it is the right size – will make a good container for your pot plants. Large urns, glass, china, jardinieres, teapots, mugs, and even kettles are possibilities.

## Making the best of a small garden

In towns, the word 'garden' is often misleading. Often the American term 'yard' would be more descriptive. Plenty of town back gardens are merely small square or rectangular patches between two rows of back-to-back terrace houses–each one, probably, with a frontage of no more than 15 feet. Sometimes, too, such a garden is found in the central well formed by an extension or as an integral part of an architect-designed complex of new housing.

These mini-gardens need treating in quite a different way from larger ones. For a start, paving almost always looks better than grass in a confined space. (A combination of children and wet grass can result, anyway, in a sea of mud in no time at all.) A scaled-down version of the conventional herbaceous border planted down one side looks not only boring but cramped. And left completely alone, such a backyard is nothing but an eyesore –

especially when seen through living room or dining room windows.

### Garden walls

Almost always, a tiny garden is enclosed; and one or two of its walls may be formed by the back or sides of another house.

This enclosure is often an advantage. High walls shut off noise, besides giving privacy – plus a lot more gardening space. But as the brickwork will be seen when the last leaf has fallen from the last creeper, it is important that walls are treated as an integral part of the garden itself.

If you wish to extend your walling, woven wooden palings (which need creosoting to protect them from the weather) are comparatively cheap, but not particularly versatile. A good brick wall is much more satisfactory. In many places, too, the heights of side walls, and the materials in which they may be built, are limited by local authority

regulations; fireproof materials are often preferred, or compulsory, when a wall is on a boundary.

Brick walls, provided they are in good repair, can be colourwashed in any of the pale, pretty, sugar-almond colours that are almost as light-reflecting as white. Although white itself is fresh and gay, it goes dirty extremely quickly; and on a grey winter's day looks cold and depressing. The hint-of-a-tint given by the admixture of pink, ochre, or turquoise – even a cupful or two to the gallon makes a difference – to the basic white paint gives a warmer, slightly 'Mediterranean' look. In warmer, crisper climates, white walls or palings look brilliant in sunlight.

This Mediterranean look can be backed up by using pretty bits of ceramics or glass – for instance, lining an alcove in the wall with tiny, brilliant blue Italian glass mosaic tiles. Then there are small, fairly cheap, weatherproof ceramic ones that could cover a project-

1 A tiny back garden made a
blaze of colour by a terrace banked high
with bright shrubs and greenery at
different levels.
2 A small yard livened up by introducing
both paved and grassed areas
surrounded by bright white walls.
3 A sophisticated angle for a corner
garden! The goldfish pool adds a cool note
to the paved outside lounge.
4 Using the subtle shades of
green against moss and mellow stone.
The light shines attractively through
the foliage.

ing ledge to make a plant table. Even an
unpromising basement area wall can be
prettied up by painting it a light, gay
colour and hanging a few random
Portuguese or Spanish patterned tiles.

A piece of mirror in the garden is
another simple but effective idea. Try a
tall one to reflect a narrow little Cypress
tree, or a squarer one angled behind an
urn full of spilling Geraniums. A gener-

ous slab of mirror on a wall behind a
wide-spaced trellis supporting a tangle
of blue Morning Glories, for example, can
appear to add yards of beauty to a tiny
garden. Be careful, though, to use the
mirror just far enough from a cultivated
area that the rain cannot splash it with
mud streaks.

## Levels

In a tiny garden, you should 'think
vertically' as well as 'thinking horizontally'. In other words, it is important
to create a series of points of interest at
different heights.

If you want to pack the garden with
plants and flowers, this means aiming for
the effect of standing in the middle of a
flower basket, with a lot of blooms at eye
or shoulder level, rather than looking
down on flat, ground-level beds, such as
you might use in a larger garden.

Achieving different flowerbed levels
usually means a lot of hard work at first.
Topsoil must be carefully removed. A

foundation of rubble, gravel, or builders'
debris must be built up and shaped into a
miniature landscape of hills and valleys,
then the topsoil replaced over this
foundation. As there will now be a
greater surface area to cover, more topsoil must either be bought, or brought up
sack by sack from the country. (Most
town topsoil is stale; so take advantage
of this preparing stage to add whatever
is needed, from moisture-retaining peat
to fertilizer.)

Once the beds are made, they can be
broken up into small separate areas by
brickwork, or paths made from flag-
stone pieces. These paths are not just
decorative: they provide firm squatting-
stones when you want to plant or weed.
Lilliputian terraces, like small fields or
vineyards descending a hill, can be
equally effective, especially with hanging or trailing plants. Brick edging can
be used here, or dry stone walling made
from pieces of flat stone, or paving chips
too small for any other use.

1 A town plot seen as a quiet
'retreat'. The fine old urn acts as
focal point, centred in paving, and the
whole area framed in greenery.
2 Hanging baskets and ground-level
flowers hide an ugly spot.
The colour is relieved by restful foliage.
3 A terrace given a distinct character
through the skilful use of stone,
evergreen and flowering shrubs.
4 Spiky and smooth shrubs provide
variety in a small garden.

## A corner for leisure

If you prefer to devote the whole of a
tiny garden to a flat space for children's
play, sitting about, or sunbathing, it
becomes even more important to concentrate a lot of the interest higher than
the basic ground level to avoid a 'walled-
up' feeling. Should you be lucky enough
to have a tree growing in one corner of
the garden, you have a ready-made solu-
tion; if not, you could plant your own
tree; concentrate on climbing plants –
perhaps growing a Vine or Wisteria right
up the side of the house; fix pots to the
walls; or site plant boxes on the top of
walls to trail foliage downwards.

## Materials

A plain sweep of lawn looks magnificent
in the open spaces of a large garden; in a
tiny one, a certain amount of cunning
and intricacy works best. Even the
Japanese, masters of the simple, single-
spray-in-a-vase school of flower arrang-
ing, avoid this approach in their tiny
gardens; each one is a balanced, but
complicated, little masterpiece.

In a paved garden, try a few con-
trasting materials. A sunburst of bricks
around a tree, a miniature patio area
near the house, covered in heather-
brown quarry tiles, or old-fashioned
cobblestones to outline or emphasize the
paving itself, add a richness to an otherwise boring area.

In Britain, beautiful old paving stones
with varying grey-gold colours and
slightly irregular surfaces can be bought
cheaply (especially if broken or damaged) from local councils who are replacing
pavement surfaces. Almost anywhere,
you can find mellow old bricks from a
house that is being demolished or con-
verted. Although this material can be
chipped or broken, and sometimes needs
hours of work to strike off old mortar, its
textured surface or matured colouring
is much more attractive than the flat
regularity of cement or concrete paving.

In a paved garden, allowance should
always be made for drainage. You can
arrange this by making a very slight
slope towards a central drainage hole or
small grid, or towards several cracks
between paving stones which are not
cemented together, but loose-filled with
gravel or sand. In this way you should
remove any excess water which could
otherwise threaten to drown your plants.

## Providing a focus

All tiny gardens need some kind of focus
– if only to remove the impression of
standing in a small square box. Trees,
water, plants, statuary, all (though not
all together!) make good focal points.

A focal-point tree should be the sort
that is a good shape even when the
branches are bare, or should be an evergreen.

Views vary on the use of water in
gardens. Streams and small lakes are
one thing; small stagnant-looking pools
covered with a floating debris of leaves
and insects are another. Part of the
charm of any garden is movement (think
of swaying branches, bird flight) so that
running water is always a delight – the
sunlit fountains in the stone courtyards
of Spanish houses are perfect examples.
Fountains may be beyond our reach,
but a birdbath is within reach of all –
perhaps an old stone one, perhaps a new
but weathered-looking fibreglass one,
placed on the edge of a banked-up
terrace bed. Plant a small shrub, some
Ferns, or a few small, bright flowers
nearby, and you almost have the effect
of a miniature pool.

Statuary, which can mean anything
from an exquisite small bronze to a stone
urn, heightens interest in any garden.
Few people can afford really superb
pieces – but anyone who can afford to
consider a piece of sculpture might
reflect that it is often seen at its best
out of doors.

There are, too, all sorts of smaller
items that enhance a small space, from
a sundial bought when an old house is
demolished to a modern fibreglass urn
whose shape and pattern are taken from
an eighteenth-century mould. Large
terracotta flowerpots, in different shapes
and sizes, are particularly flattering –
and are cheap. Even a clutch of chimney-
pots or drainpipes, of different widths
and heights, grouped together and
planted with Ivy or Geraniums, can make
a decorative and interesting focal point.

## Plants

Focal-point plants should have a very
definite shape. The stiffness of a large
Yucca, the dark formality of a little
Cypress, are good examples. Remember
that pencil-shaped trees, such as flowering Cherries, block out less light from
the rest of the garden. The sort with angular
bare branches, like Figs or Magnolias,
let light through in a dappled pattern,
as well as providing interesting shapes.

Although what can be planted in a
garden depends to a large extent on the
type of soil, climate, rainfall, and so
forth, successful planting of a small
garden depends on certain other factors
as well.

As most very small gardens are in
towns, with high walls surrounding
them, they usually get very little light
indeed. This means using plants that

thrive in dark conditions. This, in turn,
means depending on greenery rather
than blooms.

Space is usually so limited that bare
earth looks much more desolate than in
a larger garden. Coat flowerbeds between plants and shrubs with tiny,
quick-spreading ground-level green
plants; this will also stop weeds growing.

In a mini-garden, each plant is an
individual. A permanent one must pay
its way in terms of shape or foliage for
most of the year, if it is not to leave
a gap like an extracted tooth when
flowering time is over. Others may be
best planted singly, or sparingly, otherwise their effect may be to pull the rest
of the garden out of scale, when they are
not in bloom. In a tiny area, three yellow
crocuses give just as much of an effect
of spring as an orchardful in a country
garden. For brilliant colour, or scent, a
few bedding-out plants or seedlings can
be installed in chosen sites, in tubs or
urns.

## Lighting

One of the advantages of a tiny garden is
that it can so easily be floodlit. Just one
lamp, tucked beneath the house window,
and beaming on to the plants opposite,
may be all that is needed. Or it could be
set at ground level behind a statue, to
throw this and the surrounding shrubs
into relief; or spiked into a flowerbed to
illuminate some particularly decorative
bloom.

The dramatic effect of the interplay of
light and shadows in a small, lit-up
garden creates a living picture-wall for
anyone indoors in the dining or sitting
room. It is especially effective if you are
entertaining – and is, incidentally, a
burglar-deterrent.

## An extra room?

If you are short of living space, you may
wish to treat a small back garden pri-
marily as an extra living room, or as an
extension of a kitchen-dining room,
especially in warm weather. In this case
a glazed (or better still, double-glazed)
door into the garden gives a sense of
extra space and continuity where a conventional wooden door would act as a
view-stopper.

In an extra 'room' of this kind, seating
s important. Mini-gardens often belong
to smallish houses so that, while there is
plenty of attractive garden furniture
available, finding somewhere to store it
is a problem. An alternative to the white-
painted iron seat, or teak bench, that
can be left out all year round, is built-in
seating. A brick or concrete block bench
down the length of one wall can be
softened with a scatter of gingham
cushions for impromptu outdoor meals,
and double as a parking place for glasses
if you have a small drinks party – or even,
since your outdoor room is still a
garden, as a table for plant pots!

# Growing Bonsai – miniature trees

The beautiful mature bonsai (left) is a particularly fine example because its leaves and berries are in good proportion with its size. The things to look for when purchasing a bonsai are that the plant is small and attractive, that the trunk is thick in proportion to the height, that the plant and its roots look healthy and that it has small leaves. In general the slow-growing or small trees are the best sort to buy first of all – but one drawback is that as it sometimes takes 100 years to develop a mature tree then the grower is unlikely to ever see the full fruits of his labours.

Two rocks (below) give an interesting landscape to this Cypress bonsai group.

The art of growing miniature trees, which rarely exceed two feet in height, is a living art form.

The Chinese and Indians are reputed to have grown miniature trees in the eighth century A.D., but by the tenth century the Japanese had taken up and developed the idea. 'Bonsai' is, in fact, a Japanese word meaning 'trees growing in shallow containers'.

Bonsai are kept small by pruning and by keeping them in a small container which restricts their root growth. Those grown over two feet are usually left outdoors, those 1-2 feet high stand alone indoors and those less than one foot high are often grouped – two or more growing in one container.

One of the traditions of grouped bonsai is that an uneven number of trees is usually grown. This is because the Japanese regard uneven numbers as representative of longevity. A group of four trees is never grown, as the word four in Japanese is similar to the word for death.

## Which trees to choose

In general the slow-growing or small trees are best for bonsai, as you then have less of a struggle against nature. (Slow trees can take 50 years to reach 20 feet, whereas fast-growing ones can exceed 100 feet in the same time.) Evergreens are popular and vary little from season to season, but you can also grow flowering and fruit trees. (Choose those that have small fruit – crab apple as against eating apple.) The trees should have small leaves, or short needles, which do not detract from the perfect, miniature look of the tree. The leaves will be small on bonsai because of the pruning and dwarfing process but, again, if you choose a small-leaved tree you will have a head start.

Many types of tree not usually regarded as bonsai can be successfully grown in miniature form, so if you see anything that looks suitable it is worth attempting to grow it. But first find out as much as possible about the habits and soil preferences of the tree – the more you know about it the greater your chance of growing it successfully as a bonsai.

Below are listed some of the more popular bonsai. They are all reasonably hardy and easy to keep alive.

*Abies* (Conifer). This exceptionally beautiful evergreen has short needles and a trunk which is wide at the base but tapers sharply.

*Acer*. The deciduous Acer family includes *Acer Palmatum* (Maple) and *Acer Pseudo-platanus* (Sycamore) which both have attractive leaves.

*Betula* (Birch). A graceful deciduous tree with small foliage and white or silver bark.

*Chamaecyparis* (False Cypress). An evergreen which is obtainable in various forms, and has very small leaves.

*Cornus Mas* (Cornelian Cherry). A deciduous tree which has small yellow clusters of flowers in early spring and edible red oval fruit later.

*Cotoneaster*. The many varieties of this tree – both deciduous and evergreen – have small leaves, flowers and fruit.

*Fagus* (Beech). This deciduous tree has a well-shaped trunk and pale green leaves in spring. The leaves turn to russet in autumn but stay on the tree throughout the winter.

*Juniperus Communis* (Juniper). A very small-leaved evergreen.

*Lycium* (Boxthorn). A deciduous tree with small purple flowers and red berries.

*Malus* (Crab Apple). A number of varieties of this deciduous tree are suitable for bonsai. It has small red or white blooms in early summer and small colourful fruit in autumn.

*Morus Alba* (Silkworm Mulberry). With its many small flowers and dark green leaves the form of this deciduous tree is particularly good.

*Picea Abies* (Spruce). A shallow-rooted evergreen with fine-needled foliage.

*Pinus* (Pine). The most popular of the bonsai and the Japanese symbol of life.

*Prunus*. The deciduous *Prunus* family includes the *Prunus Mume* (Apricot), *Prunus Jamasakura* (Cherry) – which dislikes pruning, and *Prunus Communis* (Almond). The Apricot is perhaps the easiest to grow. Choose a small-leaved and small-flowered variety.

*Pyracantha Coccinea* (Firethorn). A deciduous tree which has small leaves, and tiny white flowers in mid-summer. These turn to yellow or red berries in autumn, and last for about five months.

*Quercus* (Oak). Another deciduous tree, oak is particularly good for bonsai as it is slow growing and has lots of branches.

*Salix* (Willow). A deciduous tree, *Salix Babylonica* (the Weeping Willow) is particularly lovely.

*Taxus* (Yew). A hardy evergreen whose trunk naturally looks gnarled as the tree grows. It also produces attractive scarlet berries.

*Tilia Europaea* (Lime). This lovely deciduous tree has red twigs, and small, pale green, heart-shaped leaves.

## To buy or to grow?

There are basically two ways of obtaining a bonsai – either you buy it or you grow it. If you buy one you lose some of the absorbing work of pruning it and determining its shape, but you do see a mature end result.

You can buy one fully grown, container and all, from a specialist nursery. Or – from autumn to spring when they are resting – you can buy one grown but 'root-wrapped' (that is, with its ball of soil protectively wrapped in some way) rather than in a container. You then plant it yourself, which means you have the choice of container.

Alternatively, as bonsai are usually rather expensive to buy, you could grow your own from a seed, seedling or cutting. Oak, Willow, Beech, Sycamore, and Conifers are easy to grow in this way if you give them enough warmth, moisture and air.

The drawback here is that it can take up to 100 years to develop a mature bonsai!

The major points to look for when buying or growing a bonsai are that the plant is small and attractive, that the trunk is thick in proportion to the height, that the plant itself and its roots look healthy, and that it has small leaves.

## How to grow bonsai

An Acorn or Chestnut will grow if you plant it. You can take a cutting from a tree. Or, if you are lucky, you may find a suitable seedling. Cuttings should be 3 inches long, cut just below a leaf node so that they can drink easily. Take soft wood cuttings in the spring, and hard wood ones in autumn, choosing wood of that year's growth.

To plant, make holes in the side and bottom of a pot. (If it is clay you will need to drill these, if plastic you can make them using a sharp knife.) Put crocks and gravel at the bottom of the pot to help drainage, then fill the pot with a sandy compost. A seed should be planted about its own height below the soil, a cutting about one third of its length, and a seedling as a plant. Leave half an inch at the top of the pot for watering.

As roots come through the holes in the pot snip them off, and after one year in the pot if it is a cutting or seedling, or two or three years for a seed, repot into its new container and, later, start pruning the top growth very carefully.

## Watering

Water bonsai about once a day, never allow the soil to dry out, but be careful not to overwater. The soil should be kept just moist at all times.

You will need to water more frequently in hot weather and in the growing season and less in winter.

The larger leafed varieties of bonsai should have their leaves sprayed occasionally. But never do this in the heat of the day or while the tree is receiving direct sunlight. Sun on water droplets has the same effect as a magnifying glass – the leaves will be burnt or scorched.

## Soil

Use different grades of coarse mixed

soil which are suitable for your particular tree, some water retentive and some open and porous. If you use too fine a soil it will clog down when watered and not enough air will be able to circulate around the roots.

Put the coarsest soil in the bottom of the pot, above the crocks, and the finest soil on top and around the roots.

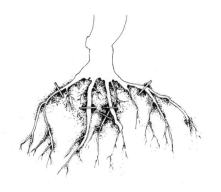

These roots should be pruned as marked

After pruning bushy new roots branch out

## Feeding

Bonsai, like pot plants, need regular feeding with a liquid fertilizer during the growing season. This is because their roots are restricted as to the area they can stretch out to in search of food.

## Repotting

This is best done in the dormant season when the plant is not growing. So, repot spring-flowering trees in autumn, deciduous trees in autumn or early spring, and conifers any time except mid-summer and mid-winter.

Young trees, obviously, need repotting more frequently than old ones as they grow more quickly. To see if a tree needs repotting look at the bottom drainage holes, if more than two or three roots are poking out then it needs repotting. (If, on the other hand, none are visible some time after repotting check the plant; it is a sign that the roots are unhealthy.)

Let the soil dry out before repotting to make it easier to remove. Loosen the soil from around the roots, then repot with dry soil as this will not clog and prevent air circulating around the roots. Water well, and then leave the tree in a protected place – in the garden if there is no danger of frost – for a few days to recover and settle in.

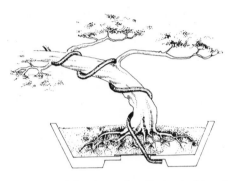

Binding with wire trains the bonsai trunk

Never wire tightly or loosely, but firmly

## Root pruning

This is done when repotting and does not, in itself, dwarf a tree – rather it promotes healthy growth. The fine roots feed the tree and the larger ones hold it firmly in the ground. Carefully knock off most of the earth, then trim the large coarse roots as, clearly, they are not really necessary to bonsai. Also remove any broken and dead roots. There should be a space of $\frac{3}{4}$-1 inch between the root ball and the side of the container.

Pruning roots in this way also helps to ensure that they get enough air. Too many roots tangled together (or heavy soil) prevent this. Remember to use a sharp tool when pruning the roots to avoid damaging or bruising them.

## Wiring

Wire is twisted around the trunk or branches of bonsai to encourage growth in a particular direction, or to develop a

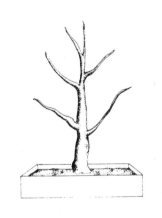
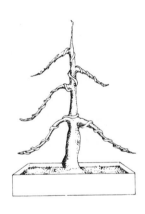

Upturned branches help a tree's looks

Correct this by wiring the branches down

gnarled-looking twist. Do not wire immediately following repotting as you must allow time for the plant to settle. Use copper wire – except for Cherry trees or young delicate shoots where pipe cleaners should be used. Do not wire unnecessarily and be careful not to damage the branch. Remove the wire as soon as the branch is set in its new position.

When wiring the trunk of the tree the end of the wire must be anchored so that it is taut enough to pull the trunk in the required direction. You can do this by inserting the wire through the drainage hole while you are repotting, and then leaving it on the surface of the soil until you are ready to wire the trunk.

## Top pruning

Bonsai are pruned to give them shape and a bushy appearance. This should generally be done in spring. Never prune roots and the top growth at the same time, as this will give the plant too much of a shock.

Cut off the top tips to get a bushy look. And prune carefully to give the tree the desired shape. Think about the final shape you want the tree to have, and consider the angle from which it will be seen. If you buy a ready-grown bonsai you will of course only have to trim it, its basic shape will have been established long before you bought it. This is another advantage with the most unusual greenery you can add to your home.

# The best plants to grow

**Euphorbia pulcherrima 'Viking', the Poinsettia, is one of the most popular of flowering plants indoors at Christmas**

## Adiantum (ad-e-an-tum)

The Greek name *adiantos*, dry, indicates the way in which water runs off the leaves or fronds (*Polypodiaceae*). Maidenhair fern. Most kinds of adiantum are from the tropics but a few are hardy or nearly hardy in Great Britain. They are well known and deservedly popular for their pale green, confetti-like foliage (pinnules) held on wiry stems.

**Greenhouse species cultivated** All these require a winter temperature of 60–70°F (16–21°C). *A. caudatum,* 9–12 inches, a tropical species to grow on high staging or in decorative baskets where the arching, pendent fronds can be shown off. Small tufts of fronds appear on the tips of established fronds which can be pegged down and layered to increase stock. *A. cuneatum,* 8–12 inches, grown commercially as the maidenhair fern of the florists. A native of Brazil with attractive varieties including *dissectum, elegans* and *gracillimum. A. williamsii,* 1 foot, from Peru, known as the golden maidenhair because of the yellow dust on the undersides of the fronds.

**Hardy species cultivated** *A. capillus-veneris,* 6 inches, which grows wild in parts of the western seaboard of the British Isles and in the Channel Isles; vars. *cornubiense* and *imbricatum* are both useful for shady crevices. *A. pedatum,* 1–1½ feet, North American maidenhair, was among the first American plants brought to Britain in 1637, having been discovered by John Tradescant; vars. *japonicum,* 3 feet, with rose-pink fronds and stems when the young growth starts, 'Klondyke', 2½ feet, found in that region at the time of the gold rush, has pink-tinged fronds. *A. venustum,* 1–2 feet, is especially good in 'Don's Canadian Form'. The pinnules are regularly and closely set giving the fronds a richer appearance than in the type.

Adiantum may also be grown as a house plant; it likes a cool situation protected from strong sunlight, ideally a window sill facing east. Daily syringing in lukewarm water is recommended, as is the deep dish method of cultivation. Repot every spring in good quality potting compost mixed with a little peat-moss. Propagate by dividing the plants at potting time; even separation into single rooted pieces is successful. Fern spores, the dark brown 'scales' on the backs of the fronds, may be sown on sterilised seed compost in a temperature of 55 F (13 C). The resulting moss-like growth produces tiny heart-shaped plants from which the miniature fronds develop.

## Aechmea (eek-me-a)

From the Greek *aichme*, a point, referring to the rigid points on the calyx (*Bromeliaceae*). Evergreens from tropical America introduced in the early nineteenth century, long grown in stovehouses, but a few species are now grown successfully as house plants.

They are distinct from many plants because the leaves spring directly from the root, overlapping in rosette fashion to form a tube, through which the flower spike emerges. The flowers are short-lived but the colourful bracts may persist for many months.

**Species cultivated** *A. fulgens,* 1½ feet, dark green leaves, purple flowers, persistent scarlet bracts; var. *discolor,* 2½ feet, from Brazil, leaves maroon-purple below, greenish-grey above, purple-blue flowers, scarlet, persistent bracts. *A. mariae-reginae,* 2 feet, blue flowers, ageing to pink, rose-pink bracts. *A. rhodocyanea (A. fasciata),* leaves 4 inches wide, 18 inches long, greyish-green banded with silver grey. Plants may be 2 feet or more across. The pink flower stem is 1½ feet tall and bears lavender-blue flowers which last for a short time only, although the spiny pink bracts remain colourful for six months or more, before it is necessary to cut off the dead rosette.

**Cultivation** The vase-like tube formed by the leaves should be kept filled with water, rainwater if available, preferably tepid in winter. In summer very dilute liquid fertiliser may be added occasionally. Watering of the compost should be reduced in winter, especially when the room temperature is low.

After flowering the rosette eventually dies but this may take six to twelve months during which time offsets will have formed which will themselves flower in due course. The dead rosette should be cut away cleanly with a sharp knife when it begins to look unsightly.

Propagation is by detaching the sucker-like offsets which arise at the side of the plant, in March, and potting them in sandy peat in a propagating case, then potting later into 6 inch pots. Compost: equal parts of fibrous loam, rough peat and leafmould. If possible maintain a winter temperature of 60–70 F (16–21 C), although *A. rhodocyanea* has proved to be surprisingly tough and will survive in much lower room temperatures provided the compost is not kept wet.

## Aglaonema (ag-lay-o-ne-ma)

From the Greek *aglaos*, bright, and *nema*, thread, probably referring to the shining stamens of the flowers (*Araceae*). Evergreen-leaved plants cultivated in pots for house and greenhouse decoration. Closely related to the calla lily (*Zantedeschia*), the flowers are not un-

like those of that plant. The foliage varies with species, some being mottled with golden-yellow or silver markings.

**Species cultivated** *A. angustifolia,* 9 inches, whitish flowers. *A. costatum,* 6 inches, white flowers July, a low growing kind useful for bottle gardens and the like. *A. modestum,* Chinese evergreen, 12–20 inches, with leaves on long stalks, thrives in poorly lighted places and is said to grow in water alone. *A. pseudobracteatum,* feather leaf, 9–12 inches, a decorative bushy species used as a house plant, golden yellow leaves marked with grey and dark green margins. Needs plenty of humidity.

**Cultivation** The compost required is made up of 2 parts of loam to 1 part of leafmould with a good scattering of sand. Plants like a shaded position and frequent watering when growing, and regular feeding with a liquid fertiliser for pot plants in spring and summer. Syringe the foliage daily in the conservatory or greenhouse. A winter temperature of 70°F (21°C) is ideal but the plants survive quite well in lower temperatures, down to 55°F (13°C) with careful watering, especially when grown as houseplants.

## Aloe (al-o-e)

The Greek name, or from the Arabic *alloch* (*Liliaceae*). Evergreen plants for greenhouse and window; some are small and suitable for room culture, others grow very tall and tree like. There are very many species and they have leaves in the form of rosettes, some are strongly toothed at the edges, others are smooth. The leaves in some species are large and leathery and others are striped with yellow markings.

**Species cultivated** As there are hundreds of species and varieties it is possible to name only a few. *A. abyssinica,* stemless, many leaves in rosettes, sword-shaped and strongly toothed, flowers numerous on tall stalks, red-yellow, Eritrea. *A. africana,* stem 6 feet high, leaves in rosettes, tough and spiny, flowers yellow to orange, Transvaal, Port Elizabeth, Port Alfred. *A. arborescens,* grows very tall (20–30 feet), makes many stems in clump, leaves horny and toothed, purple-red flowers, Cape Province. *A. aristata,* compact rosettes, very thin, pointed

leaves, lightly toothed and speckled with white, orange-red flowers, Cape Province, Natal, Orange Free State, can winter out of doors in southern England. *A. candelabrum*, tree like, stems bare low down with some dried leaves adhering near top, leaves recurved in rosettes, scarlet or orange-pink flowers, Natal, Durban. *A. claviflora*, stemless, leaves in clusters, sword-shaped and upcurved, yellowish-orange-red flowers, Bushmanland. *A. comosa*, tree-like, greenish-white flowers, Cape Province. *A. davyiana*, stemless, leaves fleshy with reddish spots on upper surface, pale pink flowers, Transvaal. *A. dichotoma*, grows to 40 feet or more, stem bare with cluster of leaves at top, bright yellow flowers, Little Namaqualand. *A. variegata*, the well known partridge-breasted aloe, a very good house plant, triangular-shaped pointed leaves, pale green with darker markings like feathers of partridge, flowers bell shaped on tall stem, greenish pink easily propagated by suckers sent up from below ground level, Namaqualand, Cape Province.
**Cultivation** A suitable compost consists

1 **Adiantum venustum** and 2 **Adiantum pedatum** are two maidenhair ferns.
3 **The lavender-blue flowers and persistent pink bracts of Aechmea rhodocyanea, a tough house plant.**
4 **The scarlet and purple of Aechmea has only a short-lived beauty.**
5 **The Partridge-breasted Aloe.**

of 2 parts of loam, 1 part of peat, 1 part of very sharp, coarse sand (river grit is best), to which should be added John Innes base fertiliser as for John Innes No. 1 potting compost (see Composts, Soil). Grow the plants in a sunny greenhouse in pots or tubs, large tubs may be stood outside greenhouse for summer. Water when soil is dry during April to September, but refrain when the weather is cold and dull; give winter's rest. Pot in March or April. Temperature: winter, 45–50°F (7–10°C), summer to 65°F (18°C). Propagation is by seeds or offsets, some species by leaf cuttings. Seed should be sown in early spring in John Innes seed compost, just covering the seed in a temperature of 70°F (21°C) for in lower temperatures seed is slow to germinate.

**Ananas** (an-a-nas)
From *nanas*, the South American name for the pineapple (*Bromeliaceae*). Grown in vast quantities commercially, pineapple plants can be grown for decoration and interest in a greenhouse. It is quite

possible to raise plants to the fruiting stage under these conditions. The fruit forms on a central spike rising from the basal rosette of spiny leaves and is best supported.

**Species cultivated** *A. comosus*, leaves 3–5 feet long, about 1½ inches wide. Flowers in a conical head, reddish violet, April; varieties include: *sativus*, flowers and fruits larger, leaves more spiny; *debilis*, wide wavy leaves, fruit long; *lucidus*, spineless leaves; *porteanus*, leaves have a broad stripe lengthwise; *variegatus*, leaves with yellow margins. The pineapple makes a decorative houseplant; the dwarf form now available is more suitable in smaller rooms.

**Cultivation** A high temperature is required at all times; winter minimum 65°F (18°C) to 90°F (32°C) summer. Water freely while growing, with high humidity. Keep drier in winter. Fruits form on 2-year-old plants. Give liquid feeds while these are developing. Keep plants on the dry side when fruits are ripening. Propagation is either by suckers separated in spring, or by rooting the leafy tops of the fruits with strong bottom heat.

## Anthurium (an-thu-re-um)

From the Greek *anthos*, flower, and *oura*, tail, referring to the spadix (*Araceae*). These evergreen tropical plants have been grown in this country since the early nineteenth century, as much for their foliage as for their flat, brilliantly coloured 'flowers' that look like broad leaves with a tail in the middle. They are very popular with flower arrangers because of their bold effect, and lasting qualities when cut. Provided they are given the right greenhouse conditions, they are easy enough to grow, forming plants about 3 feet in height. They are occasionally sold as house plants and will do reasonably well if they can be given a place in shade, out of draughts, in a warm room, preferably where the temperature does not fall below 60°F (16°C).

**Species cultivated** *Flowering: A. andreanum*, scarlet and white. *A. ornatum*, white and purple. *A. scherzerianum*, scarlet. *Foliage: A. crystallinum*, green. *A. magnificum*, white and green leaves. *A. veitchii*, green. Various cultivars are offered by specialist growers.

**Cultivation** A damp but well-drained spongy compost consisting of peat and sphagnum moss is ideal. The pots should be placed in a shady position in the greenhouse. They need a warm, humid atmosphere and should be potted in March and watered freely until November, when watering should be reduced, although the plants should not be allowed to dry out. Keep the temperature between 70–80°F (21–27°C) during the summer and 60–65°F (16–18°C) in the winter months. The roots may be divided in spring or seeds may be sown in a

compost of sand, charcoal and chopped sphagnum moss in a temperature of 80°F (27°C) in spring.

## Aphelandra (af-el-an-dra)

From the Greek *apheles*, simple, and *andros*, male, referring to the one-celled anthers (*Acanthaceae*). Evergreen shrubs from the tropics which must be grown in a hothouse in this country although one is a popular house plant. The bracts surrounding the flowers overlap one another giving the flower head a sculptured appearance.

**Species cultivated** *A. aurantiaca*, 3 feet, orange flower-heads. *A. pectinata*, 3 feet,

1 Ananas comosus is a form of pineapple which may be grown indoors.
2 Anthurium andreanum.

scarlet. *A. squarrosa*. 3 feet, dark-green, ivory-banded leaves, yellow flower-heads, greenish-yellowish bracts; var. *louisae*, in which the leaves have ivory-white midribs and more distinctive ivory bands, is grown as a house plant. *A. tetragona*, 3 feet, scarlet.

**Cultivation** Grow these plants in pots in a moist atmosphere in a compost of peat, loam, leafmould and sand in equal parts. Summer temperature should be 70–80°F (21–27°C); slightly less in winter. Water

freely in summer, sparingly in winter. Repot in March and prune in February, cutting the shoots to within 1 inch of their base. Propagate by cuttings rooted over bottom heat in a sandy compost in March or April. When grown in the house, *A. squarrosa louisae* does not need a high room temperature, 50°F (10°C) is adequate. It needs moderate watering in winter which should be increased when growth begins in the spring, when the plant should be repotted, using John Innes potting compost No. 3. Potbound plants flower more readily; feeding should not begin until the flower buds appear.

## Aporocactus (a-por-o-kak-tus)
From the Greek *aporos*, impenetrable, but for no obvious reason (*Cactaceae*). Greenhouse plants with drooping, spine-covered stems up to 2 feet long. *A. flagelliformis* is the well-known 'rat-tailed cactus', suitable for window culture and hanging baskets.

**Species cultivated** *A. flagelliformis*, rat-tailed cactus, slender stems with fine spines, cerise-pink flowers in spring, Peru. *A. martianus*, stems erect or sprawling, flowers red to scarlet with violet edge, Mexico. *A. × mallisonii*, hybrid between *A. flagelliformis* and *Heliocereus speciosus*, large bright red flowers.

**Cultivation** A suitable growing medium is John Innes potting compost No. 2, to which should be added a fifth part of sharp, coarse sand with broken brick included. Repot every two or three years, give light stimulants when in bud; give plenty of light at all times and sun whenever possible. These plants can take more water than many cacti but soil must be well drained. Temperature minimum 40°F (4°C) in winter when plants must be kept dry, 70°F (21°C) in summer.

Propagation is by seeds sown in sandy soil in spring; cover them by their own depth only and keep them moist and warm. Cuttings of young shoots may also be used for propagation, dry these before placing them on sharp sand and peat in equal quantities; do not push cuttings into this or they may rot; aerial roots often form on the stems.

## Asparagus (as-par-ag-us)
The prickles on some species are said to give this genus its name, from the Greek *a*, intensive, and *sparasso*, to tear (*Liliaceae*). A genus which includes perennial climbers and shrubs for the greenhouse as well as a vegetable for the epicure. The greenhouse species with their diversity of fine foliage are invaluable to the florist. They also make excellent pot plants and are specially useful for hanging baskets. The hardy herbaceous asparagus has feathery foliage which

**Aphelandra squarrosa louisae is an excellent flowering house plant. When the plant is not in flower the ivory-ribbed leaves are handsome**

grows to about 4 feet, but this species is grown for the plump young shoots which are cut for eating when they are about 4 inches long.

**Greenhouse species cultivated** *A. aspara-goides*, climber to 10 feet, known as smilax by the florist. *A. plumosus*, climber to 10 feet, very fine foliage and known as asparagus fern, used extensively in bouquets. There is also a dwarf variety, *nanus*. *A. sprengeri*, climber to 6 feet, a good species for hanging baskets.

## Aspidistra (as-pe-dis-tra)

The flowers are shield-like and this may be the origin of the name from the Greek *aspidior*, a little shield (*Liliaceae*). Aspidistras are nearly hardy evergreen pot plants for the living-room or greenhouse. Their great asset is that they will tolerate unsuitable conditions such as dark, sunless living-rooms. They are grown for their foliage, the leaves being broad and emerging from soil level. The species grown is *A. lurida* (syn. *A. elatior*) known by the popular name of parlour palm or cast-iron plant because it will put up with a great deal of neglect and still survive. There is a striped variety, called *variegata*, in which the dark-green leaves are irregularly striped with creamy-white.

**Cultivation** Any good potting compost such as a mixture of loam and leafmould will suit the aspidistra. Water it throughout the year and sponge the leaves when necessary, to remove any dust. The

plants may be divided when they become
overcrowded and any repotting should
be done in the spring. These plants do
not require any heat but they must be
kept away from frost.

## Asplenium (as-ple-ne-um)

From the Greek *a*, not and *splene*, spleen,
referring to the fact that one species was
once regarded as a cure for diseases of
the spleen (*Polypodiaceae*). Spleenwort.
A large genus of ferns, hardy and tender,
widely distributed throughout the world,
varying in size from a few inches to as
much as 6 feet.

**Hardy species cultivated** A. *adiantum-
nigrum*, black spleenwort, 9–12 inches, a
native, good for walls, hedge-banks or
rock garden. A. × *breynii*, a hybrid, 4
inches, found wild in Britain. A. *ruta-
muraria*, 2–3 inches, the wall fern, another native, good for the shady side of a
rock garden. A. *trichomanes*, maidenhair
spleenwort, 6–12 inches, a native with
several varieties. A. *viride*, 3–6 inches,
green spleenwort, likes a moist place.

**Greenhouse** A. *bulbiferum*, fronds up to
2 feet long, 1 foot broad. A. *colensoi*, 6–9
inches, bears young plants along the
fronds. A. *dimorphum*, 2–3 feet. A. *inci-
sum*, 6–12 inches. A. *platyneuron*, narrow fronds, 2–3 feet long.

**Stovehouse** A. *nidus*, the bird's nest
fern, has undivided fronds up to 4 feet
long and 6–9 inches broad.

**Cultivation: Hardy species** The small
species make good plants for the rock
garden and for crevices in old walls, but
most of them like a little shade. The
larger species do well at the foot of a wall
or in a shady border provided it is fairly
moist. Add some leafmould and sand
when planting. Propagate by spores or
by division of the clumps in spring.

**Greenhouse species** Use a compost of
peat, loam, leafmould and sand in equal
parts and carry out potting in the spring.

Keep well watered in summer, moderately in winter. The temperature should be
about 75 F (24 C) for stovehouse species
and 60 F (16 C) for the greenhouse
species in the summer, lowering it 10 F
(5–6 C) or so in the winter. Propagate by
spores sown in sand and peat at any time
of the year.

## Astrophytum (as-tro-fi-tum)

From the Greek *aster*, star, *phytos*,
plant, referring to the shape of the plant
(*Cactaceae*). Star cactus. Formerly included in *Echinocactus*, these cacti mostly have globular stems, some deeply
ridged with from four to eight ribs. Flowers are produced from areoles at the top
of the plant. A well-grown specimen produces flowers at each areole as formed.

**1 Asparagus plumosus climbs to all of 10
feet and is usually known as asparagus
fern 2 Asplenium adiantum-nigrum
grows up to one foot high and is
excellent for walls.**

There are four species and many cultivars produced through crossing.

**Species cultivated** *A. asterias*, round and almost ribless, flowers yellow, large, with red centre. *A. capricorne*, ribbed with strong, curved spines, flowers yellow. *A. myriostigma*, bishop's cap, spineless, flowers yellow. *A. ornatum*, many curling spines, flowers lemon-yellow. All these are natives of Mexico.

**Cultivation** Astrophytums should be given a very porous soil with added lime. A suitable compost consists of 2 parts of loam, 1 part of peat and 1 part of sharp, coarse sand. Add 1 ounce of ground chalk and ¼ pound of John Innes base fertiliser to each bushel. Re-pot only every four years except seedlings which may be re-potted every year. Water from April to September, after which the soil is kept quite dry; never allow soil to remain wet for long periods or the plant will rot.

Give as much sun as possible at all times; there is no limit to warmth these plants can stand in summer. The temperature in winter should not fall below 40 F (4 C). As these plants never produce off-sets normally they must be grown from seed. The seeds are large with a hollow side like a cowrie shell. Sow them in John Innes seed compost, just pressing the seed in. They may germinate in 48 hours at a temperature of 70 F (21 C). Prick out when the cotyledon (seed-leaf) has been absorbed.

**Begonia** (be-go-ne-a)
Commemorating Michel Bégon, 1638–1710, Governor of Canada, patron of botany (*Begoniaceae*). These half-hardy herbaceous and sub-shrubby plants are natives of moist tropical countries, apart from Australia. They need greenhouse treatment, though a large number are now used in summer bedding schemes.

The genus begonia is usually divided into two groups; those species with fibrous roots and those with tubers. Other classifications give special treatment to the winter-flowering forms, and to those grown exclusively for the interest of their leaves. A notable feature of begonias is their oblique, lop-sided or uneven sided leaves.

There has been so much hybridising in this genus that the naming has become quite complicated, and the custom of giving Latin specific names has not made matters easier.

The begonia, unlike the majority of plants, has, instead of hermaphrodite blooms, separate male and female blossoms on the same plant; the female flowers are generally removed as not being of much interest, though if seed is required, they must, of course, be retained. The seed

1 Astrophytum myriostigma is called Bishop's Cap because of its shape. Astrophytums should be given a very porous soil with added lime. They love sunlight and should be exposed as much as possible, even in summer.
The double-flowered begonias 2 and 3 are two examples of the large-flowered hybrids. 'Flamingo' 4 is one of a number of Begonia semperflorens types often used for summer bedding. The Rex Begonias 5 are grown for their leaf colour.

is dust-fine and needs no covering of soil, in fact the raising of begonias from seed has something in common with the art of raising ferns from spores.

**Species cultivated** The best-known begonias are the hybrids of the tuberous species: *B. boliviensis, B. clarkei, B. cinnabarina, B. davisii, B. pearcei, B. rosaeflora, B. veitchii.*

Another important group consists of the hybrids and varieties of *B. rex*, a plant from Assam with most interesting, colourful foliage. The winter-flowering and fibrous-rooted varieties derived from *B.* 'Gloire de Lorraine', a variety originally raised in France in 1891 by the plant breeder Victor Lemoine, who crossed *B. socotrana* and *B. dregei,* form a most valuable group as they furnish the greenhouse at a difficult time of the year.

Fibrous-rooted species include: *B. acutifolia*, white, spring. *B. angularis*, white-veined leaves. *B. coccinea*, scarlet, winter. *B. evansiana*, pink, almost hardy (possibly hardy in the south-west). *B. fuchsioides*, scarlet, winter. *B. froebelli*, scarlet, winter. *B. foliosa*, white and rose, summer. *B. glaucophylla*, pink and pendulous, winter. *B. haageana*, pink, autumn. *B. hydrocotylifolia*, pink, summer. *B. incarnata*, rose, winter. *B. manicata*, pink, winter. *B. scharffiana*, white, winter. *B. semperflorens*, rose (has important large-flowered vars.). *B. socotrana*, pink, winter.

Nurserymen's catalogues contain long lists of hybrids of the above, too numerous to mention here, but in various shades of pink, red, cream and white with enormous double flowers in a number of different forms.

Species with ornamental leaves include: *B. albo-picta, B. argenteo-guttata*, white and pink speckled leaves. *B. heracleifolia*, leaves deeply lobed. *B. imperialis*, velvety-green leaves. *B. boeringiana*, foliage purplish and green. *B. maculata*, foliage spotted white. *B. masoniana*, ('Iron Cross'), leaves green with a prominent dark 'iron cross' marking, popular as a houseplant. *B. metallica*, foliage has metallic lustre. *B. olbia*, bronze leaves spotted white. *B. rex*, foliage metallic silver and purple. *B. ricinifolia*, bronze leaves. *B. sanguinea*, leaves blood-red beneath. There are, in addition to the species given, many hybrids with beautiful leaves, especially named garden hybrids derived from *B. rex* and its varieties and other species, all known as Rex begonias.

**Cultivation** The fibrous-rooted begonias are usually obtained from seed, which should be sown in January in a temperature of 60° F (16° C). It is also possible to root growths from the base of the plant. The sub-shrubby perennial forms will come easily from normal cuttings, or all begonias may be raised by leaf cuttings. Leaf cuttings are single leaves which are pegged down in sandy compost, the undersides of all the main veins having

been nicked with a razor blade. The
temperature should be around 60–70°F
(16–21°C). Little plants should form
where veins were cut, and these may
later be detached and potted-on separately. Most begonias need a winter
temperature of about 60°F (16°C). The
ornamental Rex type must not be exposed to full sunlight, and many of the
other classes will be happy with much
less light than suits other greenhouse
plants.

The tuberous begonias may, of course,
be grown from tubers. These are usually
started into growth by placing them in
shallow boxes of peat or leafmould in
February or March, hollow side uppermost, in a temperature of 60–70°F
(16–21°C). After roots have formed the
tubers are potted up in small pots and
later moved into larger ones. A compost
of equal parts of loam, leafmould, well-
rotted manure and silver sand is suitable. Do not start to feed these tuberous
plants till they have formed roots, or
they will decay, but after they are rooted
a bi-weekly dose of liquid manure is
helpful. The tuberous begonias may also
be raised from seed, and if this is sown in
February plants may flower from July to
October.

Tuberous begonias when their season
is over must be gradually dried out. They
may be left in their pots in a frost-proof
shed, or knocked-out and stored in clean
dry sand.

## Beloperone (bel-o-per-o-ne)

From the Greek *belos*, an arrow, *peronne*, a hand, a reference to the shape of part of the anther (*Acanthaceae*). Evergreen tender shrubs, some needing stovehouse treatment. The stove plants are natives of Brazil, but *B. guttata* from Mexico makes an interesting room plant.

**Species cultivated** *B. atropurpurea*, 3 feet, purple. *B. guttata*, shrimp plant, 2–3 feet, the reddish bracts which enclose the white blossoms and which remain decorative for a long period, give this plant its popular name. *B. oblongata*, 3 feet, rosy purple. *B. violacea*, 3 feet, violet.

**Cultivation** Pot the plants in equal parts of sand, leafmould and loam. These plants need shading from direct sunlight, although when *B. guttata* is grown in the house it should be given a position on a window-sill but out of the sun. In the greenhouse they should have a winter temperature of 45–50°F (7–10°C) and a summer temperature of 60–70°F (16–21°C).. In summer water them generously, but in winter less water is needed. If it is desired to keep these shrubs dwarfed it will be necessary to pinch out the ends of the growing shoots. Cuttings put in

1 The ruffled flowers of 'Hercules'.
2 Begonia masoniana, or 'Iron Cross'.
3 Begonia fuchsioides and 4 'Lady Roberts' both bloom in winter greenhouses.
5 Beloperone guttata, the Shrimp plant, with its colourful flower bracts.
6 'Mrs Heal' another winter begonia.

sandy soil and given a temperature of 75°F (24°C) may be readily rooted in February or later, although *B. guttata* often flowers so freely from the end of the shoots that it is not easy to find unflowered shoots with which to make cuttings.

## Billbergia (bil-ber-je-a)

Named after a Swedish botanist, J. G. Billberg (*Bromeliaceae*). Stovehouse, evergreen flowering plants with stemless, thick, fleshy leaves. The brilliant colouring of the bracts is the outstanding feature. Found from Mexico to southern Brazil.

**Species cultivated** *B. bakeri* (syn. *B. pallescens*), 18 inches, flowers green and violet, bracts long bright rose. *B. iridifolia*, 18 inches, drooping spikes of red and yellow flowers, tipped blue, bracts crimson, March. *B. lietzei*, 1 foot, rosy-pink, bracts pink. *B. morelii*, 1 foot, blue, pink and rose, bracts deep red-rose. *B. nutans*, 18 inches, yellowish-green with blue margins, bracts pink. This is the most popular species and may be grown in a cool greenhouse or as a houseplant. *B. zebrina*, 1 foot, greenish-yellow, bracts pale salmon. *B. × windii*, 1–1½ feet, pale green, blue-tipped flowers, with light red bracts. Like *B. nutans* it may be grown in a cool greenhouse or as a houseplant.

**Cultivation** Pot in March in a compost of equal parts of fibrous loam, rough peat, leafmould and silver sand. Water freely always, but good drainage is essential. Winter temperature 60–70°F (16–21°C), and from March to September 65–80°F (18–27°C). Propagation is by large-sized offshoots, inserted singly in small pots containing sandy peat in April in a temperature of 85°F (30°C). *B. nutans* grows rapidly, producing many offsets, and may need repotting every second or third year. Recent experience shows that this species will survive much lower winter temperatures, down to 40°F (4°C) or less, provided it is kept dry.

## Bromeliads

The family *Bromeliaceae* consists of some 51 genera and over 1000 species, mainly from tropical America and the Caribbean. A typical bromeliad has a rosette of leaves, often spiny, with cup-like space in the centre which usually contains water. It is commonly called the 'vase' and should be kept filled with tepid water, preferably rainwater. Bromeliads require a lot of water and this natural reservoir should be kept topped up, and water should also be given to the roots. During the growing season mild liquid manure should be given about every third week. A little of this may be put in the vase. Many bromeliads have showy bracts and remain in flower for a long time.

Some, such as *Billbergia zebrina*, with its leathery leaves marked with silver bands and its drooping head of pale

salmon bracts and greenish flowers, and *Aechmea rhodocyanea*, its grey-green leaves forming a large rosette, from which rises a substantial spike of pink bracts around lavender-blue flowers, have been popular houseplants on the Continent for years. These and other bromeliads are now more widely grown in this country, thanks to beautiful displays at leading flower shows.

Some members of the family are epiphytes, that is, they grow on other plants, particularly trees, or on rocks or other objects. Such specimens may be seen flourishing in botanic gardens, rather than in private greenhouses.

Many of the bromeliads, for example, the pineapple, *Ananas comosus* (Brazil), make large plants, but there is a good selection of colourful smaller species now available as pot plants for the greenhouse and as houseplants. When bromeliads have finished flowering the

old plant dies, but young offshoots are formed around the rosette. These will develop best if left attached to the parent plant for as long as possible.

**Cultivation** Offsets should be potted in a compost of leafmould, sphagnum moss and peat, one-third part of each. Keep the little vase full of water. Root formation will be encouraged when the temperature is between 70–80 F (21–27 C), and the offsets are kept shaded. Once the offsets are well rooted they can be given slightly cooler conditions and more light, but not full sun under glass. Established plants in a living room should have plenty of light. Plants with dark green or mottled leaves need more shading during the spring and summer than those with red, purple, or variegated leaves. Bromeliads take three or more years from seed to flowering-size plants. Fresh seed should be sown in a temperature of about 80 F (27 C). Old

seed is quite unreliable. Sow in an acid soil consisting of peat and osmunda fibre, or leafmould with a layer of sharp sand on top. The seed is scattered thinly on the surface of the soil, which should be sterilized, and just watered in. Cover the pans with a sheet of shaded glass. Germination should take about three weeks.

**Browallia** (brow-al-le-a)
Commemorating either Johan Browallius, Bishop of Abs, or Dr John Browall of Sweden *(Solanaceae)*. Annual and perennial plants from South America, usually grown as greenhouse plants. In a sheltered garden the annual species may be bedded out in early June. **Species cultivated** *B. americana* (syn. *B. demissa, B. elata),* 1–1½ feet, soft violet-blue, June to October, annual. *B. grandiflora,* 2 feet, blue with yellow tube, July, annual, Peru. *B. speciosa,* 1½–2 feet, blue, violet or white, perennial greenhouse plant usually grown as an annual,

**Various kinds of bromeliads: 1 Billbergia nutans 2 Vriesia tesselata 3 Aechmea rhodocyanea. 4 Neoregelia carolinae tricolor. 5 Browallia speciosa makes a handsome flowering pot plant.**

Colombia. *B. viscosa,* 1–1½ feet, violet-blue, white centre, summer, perennial in the greenhouse.

**Cultivation** Sow the seed in March in finely sifted soil, only just covering it, and germinate in a temperature of 55–65°F (13–18°C). When large enough to handle transplant three or four seedlings to a 5 inch pot and stand the pots on the greenhouse shelf. Give weak manure water during May and June. Pinch plants back to make them bushy. They will flower from July onwards. Seedlings for planting outdoors must be well hardened off before planting in June.

### Bryophyllum (bry-of-il-um)

From the Greek *bryo,* to sprout, and *phyllon,* leaf, a reference to the fact that the leaves bear plantlets round their edges *(Crassulaceae).* Greenhouse succulent plants which grow tall and the leaves produce small plantlets at the notches. They are easy to grow and flower even on a window sill. One plant can drop hundreds of small plantlets in a season. The flowers are produced in late autumn or early winter in large umbels, long lasting. Bryophyllums are occasionally found under *Kalanchoe.*

**Species cultivated** *B. daigremontianum,* a well-known species with well-notched leaves, pale green with red markings, plantlets produced in profusion on the leaves, flowers grey-green, plants can be placed out of doors in summer. *B. tubiflora,* tall stems with many narrow tubular leaves, like small caterpillars, plantlets on ends, flowers red to violet. Both species are from Madagascar.

**Cultivation** The compost should be a porous soil, made with John Innes No. 1 potting compost, with a sixth part added of sharp sand or broken brick. Pot in March or April, water freely during warm weather, and very little in late autumn and winter. Prune the old flowering stem back to top leaves, temperature 65–75°F (18–24°C), in summer, 45 F (7 C), in winter, when kept dry. Propagation is by seeds sown on the surface of a fine tilth of John Innes seed compost, in a temperature of 70°F (21°C); do not cover seed. Shade seedlings from sun when small. The small plantlets which appear on the leaves will often form roots while still on the plant. They are easily detached to make fresh plants, the simplest form of propagation.

### Cactus cultivation

The growing and collecting of cacti has been a popular hobby in this country for many years. Their varied shapes and colours together with the coloured spines make them fascinating and their spectacular flowers are an added interest for the grower. Some of the larger types may not flower in this country owing to the lack of intense sunshine, but many hundreds of other species should flower every year.

**Flowering cacti** Some species flower the year after the seed has been sown, while very many more can produce flowers within two years. As the native habitats of these plants are arid regions it is essential that they be allowed all the sunshine possible to enable them to grow at their best. Most cacti come from Mexico and the southern States of the USA, and also from many countries in South America, including Peru, Paraguay, Uruguay, Chile and Brazil. A few are found in the West Indies but none in Africa, India or anywhere in the east.

**Defining cacti** All cacti are succulents but not all succulents are cacti. Spines are found on all true cacti and these spines grown from a small tuft of hair or wool. This is known as an areole and no other plant has it (see Areole). No cacti have leaves except the genus *Pereskia.* This plant has areoles and leaves and also a multiple flower, unlike true cacti which have a simple or single flower. The flowers of cacti have no stem or

stalk, the ovary being connected directly with the plant. Exceptions to this rule are the Pereskias.

The flowers of most cacti are formed at the areole but a few genera produce flowers away from this point. Plants of the genus *Mammillaria* produce their flowers at the axil, the spot between the tubercles. This genus also makes new plants or offsets at the axil as well, whereas most cacti make offsets at an areole. The flowers of cacti vary considerably in size from ⅓ inch in some mammillarias to 14 inches across in some of the night-flowering types. The larger flowers may not be produced in profusion but some of the cacti with smaller flowers can have rings of flowers all round the top of the plants for months at a time.

Cacti are often described as desert plants but this is not quite true. Many are found in prairie type country where there may be a few small trees and shrubs with coarse grasses intermingled.

**1**

**5**

**2**

**6**

**3**

**7**

**4**

**8**

Some are found in good loam while others are found growing on rocks and the mountain side. Some of the best flowering cacti, the epiphyllums, grow in the forests of Brazil, usually on trees. Such cacti are classed as epiphytes or epiphytic cacti.

As cacti vary so much in size from perhaps 1 inch to 30 feet or more there are many species available to the grower to suit almost any situation or condition. Although the best place to grow a collection of cacti is in a sunny greenhouse, there are many kinds which can be grown quite well in a sunny window.

Although all cacti can go for long periods without water, it is essential that they are provided with an adequate supply during the growing period or they cannot flourish.

To grow cacti well and flower them it is imperative to provide them with a porous soil as the roots soon rot if they are wet for days on end. Many types of potting soils have been used and recommended, even different ones for each genus; it is possible, however, to grow practically all types of cacti in one kind of potting compost. The art of growing cacti is in the watering and the amount given can vary according to the type of compost. Plants can only obtain their nourishment in a liquid form and so if little water is given the plant cannot obtain too much food.

**Potting composts** A very good potting compost for cacti may be made up from John Innes potting compost No. 1, to which is added a sixth part of coarse sand to make it more porous. Some additions of broken brick or granulated charcoal may be incorporated in the added sand. If it is desired to mix a compost for general use, the following will be found quite reliable. Take 2 parts of loam, 1 part of peat and 1 part of sharp, coarse sand. Mix well and to each bushel add $\frac{3}{4}$ oz of ground chalk or limestone, $\frac{3}{4}$ oz sulphate of potash, $1\frac{1}{2}$ oz of superphosphate and $1\frac{1}{2}$ oz of hoof and horn grist. All the globular and columnar types of cacti may be grown in

**Bryophyllum tubiflorum (opposite page) attracts attention because of the way that tiny plantlets gather on the ends of its attractive leaves. These eventually drop off and are easily rooted to form a ready means of increasing the numbers of the plant. Easy stages (this page) in cultivating the very popular cactus. Originating mainly from central America, cacti have to have a porous soil for growth. 1 Preparing a pot before sowing cactus seeds. 2 Sowing the seeds. 3 The seedlings have appeared. 4 Crocking a pot for drainage before pricking out the seedlings. 5 Pricking out the tiny seedlings. 6 Potting a larger specimen with a spoon to put compost around the plant. 7 Firming the soil. 8 Grafting.**

this compost, while for the epiphytes some John Innes potting compost No. 2, may be used, as these plants will benefit from the richer soil. The very spiny types of cacti do not require heavy feeding with fertilisers and as long as they are repotted at least every two years they will grow quite well. If these plants are fed too liberally they will become lush, open in texture, and be very liable to rot off in the winter. Also it will be found that the spines formed when the plant has been fed with fertilisers may not be as stout and well coloured as if the plant had been grown harder. When making up the cactus compost it is very important to find a good loam as a basis for the mixture. An ideal type is the top spit from an old-standing meadow. Unfortunately these meadows are becoming few and far between and the loam is often only the under spit after the top turf has been removed. The peat is not so important but the sand must be very sharp and coarse. Silver sand is useless for cactus compost and the type known as washed grit, or river grit is the best.

The potting compost should not be used immediately after it has been mixed and a lapse of a fortnight at least is desirable before potting. The time to repot varies considerably, being determined by many factors. Some cacti are very slow growers and so may be left in their pots for two or three years while others may need a move twice a year. Many cacti never flower because they have been in the same stale, worn-out soil for many years. With fairly frequent watering during the growing period the roots of the plant use up the nourishment in the soil, and clearly there can be little food value left in it after about a year.

**Repotting** The best time for repotting is during the growing period, which with most cacti will be between March and September. Once new growth is seen on a plant it can be repotted. When dealing with a fairly large collection it will be found better to make a start with the larger pots. These can then be cleaned for use with other plants which may need a bigger pot. It is also a good plan to make a clear place in the greenhouse and place all repotted plants there so that none may be missed. The pots should be clean and well crocked. It is unnecessary to place a large number of crocks in the pot as they will only take up valuable space which would be better occupied by good soil. The best way to crock a pot for a cactus is to cut as large a piece of broken flower pot as will lie in the bottom of the pot. This large crock will then form a kind of platform when the plant is removed the next time. If a stick is pushed up through the drainage hole the crock will force the whole ball of soil up in the pot, whereas if a number of small pieces of crock are used it is possible to damage the roots when trying to remove the plant another time.

**Cacti and other succulents offer the enthusiast remarkable variety not only in flower colour but also in habit of growth**

Place some of the coarsest particles of compost over the crock and then a little soil. Remove the plant from the old pot and hold it by the root system. Gently work all the old soil away from the roots. If any appear dead they should be cut away. Now rest the plant in the pot and gradually work in some fresh compost. Because most of the plants are spiny it may not be possible to work the soil in with the hands as is possible with ordinary plants. A tablespoon can be used to insert the soil and it can be gently firmed in with an old table-knife handle. A wooden stick must not be used as it would catch in the spines and break them. Once a spine is broken it will never grow again. See that the plant is in the same relative position in the soil as it was before. See also that at least ½ inch of space is left at the top of the pot for watering. The plant should look right in the new pot; do not use one too large so that the plant looks lost or yet one so small that there is no room for soil as well as the base and roots of the plant. For the globular kinds of cacti a pot which is ½ inch bigger all round than the plant will do for pots up to 3½ inches in diameter, but for a larger plant a pot at least 1 inch larger all round must be provided. This will not be sufficient for many of the taller growing types as the pot must be large enough to form a firm base to stop the plant and pot from falling over.

Plastic pots may be used, especially for small plants; they do not appear to dry out as quickly as clay pots. Once the plant is potted it is important to insert the label, and a good plan is to put the date of repotting on the back. This is a useful guide in a large collection. As it is essential that the soil should be able to discharge all surplus water as soon as possible, the pots should not be stood on a flat surface. Some coarse gravel makes an ideal base on which to stand the pots. If slats are provided in the greenhouse it is better to cover them with corrugated asbestos sheeting on which the gravel may be placed. Any plants stood on shelves must have a saucer containing gravel under them to allow the free removal of surplus water.

**Watering cacti** Watering the plants presents the most important part of cactus culture. More plants are lost through overwatering than from any other cause. As has been stated before, cacti will not grow without water but if they get too much they can soon die. Newly potted cacti should not need watering for about a week. The potting soil should have been crumbly moist at the time of moving the plant. If it is too wet or too dry it cannot be firmed in the correct manner. The whole secret of watering can be described in one sentence. Never water a plant if the soil is still damp. It is not easy to tell when a cactus needs watering. Ordinary plants soon show by drooping leaves when water is required, but cacti cannot show their needs in this way. The condition of the top of the soil will indicate when water is needed. After a hot day the soil may appear dry, but this may only be the top inch. If pots are inspected in the mornings the soil should be of a uniform dampness throughout.

Rain water is better than tap water but if rain water is not available let some tap water stand in the open for a day or two before it is used. Water may be given from a can with a small spout so that it can be directed into any pot. Do not water by immersion except for the first watering after the winter. If plants are watered this way often, all the nourishing matter will soon be washed out of the pot. Cacti may be sprayed in the evening of a hot day. No water need be given from the end of September to early March. Then water when the soil has dried out, not before. The Christmas cactus, *Zygocactus truncatus*, may be watered during the winter as long as the temperature is not below 50 F. Other cacti may be left at 40 F, so that they get a winter's rest.

**Taking cuttings** Propagation is by cuttings, taking offsets or by seed raising. Cuttings taken from opuntias and epiphyllums are removed with a sharp knife and the cut part is allowed to dry in the sun. The cuttings are then rested on a mixture of equal parts of peat and sharp sand (not silver sand). Cactus potting compost may be used to fill three quarters of the pot, with the rooting medium on top. Place in a sunny position and spray occasionally. Too much water must not be given until roots have formed. Tall cuttings will have to be supported by a stick, as they must not be pushed into the medium.

**Grafting** Grafting may be done to assist the growth of a small, slow-growing type. A tall type is used for the stock, such as *Trichocereus spachianus*. The top is cut from the stock where the growth is new and healthy. The scion is cut at the base so that it is about the size of the top of the stock. It is brought in contact with the freshly cut stock and kept in position with two small weights on a piece of string, pressing the scion down firmly. Keep in the shade for a week or two and a firm joint will form.

**Raising cacti from seed** Some cacti never make offsets and these have to be raised from seed. A small propagating frame can easily be made and heated with an electric cable or even an electric lamp. Half-pots of about 4 inches in diameter are very good for sowing small quantities of seed. They can even be divided with celluloid labels if more than one species is to be sown in the pot. Use John Innes seed compost and sieve a small quantity through a perforated zinc sieve. Place the coarse material over the crock and then top up with ordinary compost, having an inch of the fine soil on top. Small seed must not be buried, but fairly large seeds can be just pushed into the soil. Water the first time by standing in containers of water so that the whole soil can be well moistened. Place in the

1 Mammillaria geminispina. 2 Aporocactus flagelliformis, the Rat-tailed Cactus. Both these are easy to grow on a sunny window-sill and should produce flowers regularly each year

frame with a piece of glass on top and then cover with dark paper. The best time to sow is in early spring, in a temperature of 70 F (21 C); seeds will germinate at a lower temperature but will take longer to do so. Once seedlings have appeared, the paper must be removed and the glass should be raised slightly. The seedlings must be kept from the direct sun for the first year but they must have plenty of light or they will become drawn. Do not allow the seed pots to dry out while germination is taking place; watering may be done with a fine spray.

Prick out when the cotyledon or food-bag has been absorbed. Before this the root is so tiny that it can be broken very easily, in which case the seedling would die. The seedlings may be placed 1 inch apart in the cactus compost as described above. Do not pot up too soon into small pots as these dry out very quickly. Boxes made of concrete or plastic are better for the seedlings until they are ready to go into 2 inch pots.

**Summer treatment** Cacti may be planted out in beds from June to September.

If they are removed from their pots it may be quite impossible to put them back in the same sized pots in the late summer or autum. They may be left in their pots, but the drainage hole must be freed from soil when they are removed. A few cacti may stand the winter out of doors but a very severe winter would probably kill them. If the grower wishes to experiment, he should make sure that any cacti left out during the winter are those which can be parted with, and not specimen plants.

All the spiny types of cacti can stand plenty of sunshine as long as there is plenty of air available in a greenhouse. The epiphytes benefit from shade during the hotter months of the year, and may be stood outside the greenhouse provided no frosts are forecast. Cacti kept in windows of the house must be where they can get the maximum amount of light and they will not flower well unless they can get a fair amount of sunshine.

Most cacti flower in spring, summer or autumn, and it will be found that many flower on new growth only. If the flowers are pollinated many colourful seed pods can be formed. On the mammillarias these pods can look very attractive.

**Miniature cactus gardens** Cacti are very suitable for miniature gardens. The bowl need not have drainage holes provided it is not overwatered. Place some crocks in the bottom and only half fill with a porous soil. When the plants are in position the rest of the soil may be added and firmed. If the soil under a flat stone, pressed into the top of the soil, is damp do not water.

**Pests** If cacti are grown well they suffer little disease but there are a few pests which may attack a sick plant. The most frequent one is mealy bug. This appears in a small tuft of wool or powder. Scale may also attack some cacti and looks like a small scab. Red spider may be a nuisance if the atmosphere is too dry. All these pests can be killed with malathion, used as directed on the bottle.

**Choosing cacti** Many species of cacti from the following genera grow well on a window ledge: chamaecereus, echinopsis, epiphyllum, gymnocalycium, lobivia, mammillaria, notocactus, opuntia, rebutia and zygocactus. A few of the smaller types of cereus can be grown and *Cleistocactus strausii* will also grow for many years before it gets too large. The dwarf types of opuntias, such as *Opuntia microdasys*, will be suitable (see their respective entries).

For planting in bowl gardens any of the small plants of the above genera will be a good choice but not the epiphyllums unless they are very small. If any of the plants grow too large for the bowl they can be removed and replaced by a smaller specimen. A suitable collection in a bowl can last for many years without it being necessary to change any plant at any time at all.

1, 2, 3, Three kinds of Caladium; tuberous-rooted plants, grown in moist warm conditions for their decorative arrow-shaped leaves, that may be taken into the house during the summer.

## Caladium (kal-a-de-um)

Said to be from the Indian or West Indian name *(Araceae)*. A genus of tuberous-rooted, deciduous perennials from tropical South America, mainly Brazil. The large arrow-shaped leaves are handsome and are borne on stems from 6–18 inches high. They vary in colour from green to cream, some with red markings and patterns, others being bright red. They thrive in a warm, moist greenhouse atmosphere and like plenty of light. They may be brought into the house during the summer, but are not really suitable as house plants for any length of time.

**Species cultivated** *C. bicolor*, 15–18 inches, a variable species with many good named forms. *C. humboldtii*, 9 inches, light green, centre white. *C. picturatum*, 9 inches, leaves pale on the underside and various colours on the upper surface. There are many named forms of this species. *C. schomburgkii*, 18 inches, green, spotted white, with reddish veins, pale beneath; many striking forms are grown.

**Cultivation** Pot moderately firmly in February or March, using pots just large enough to take the tubers in a compost of equal parts of turfy loam, peat, leaf-mould, old manure and silver sand. Move into larger pots in April or May. They can hardly be too warm so long as the atmosphere is moist and there is good light. When the leaves die down water should no longer be given, and the tubers should be stored from November to February at a temperature of about 60°F (16°C). Propagation is by division of the tubers in early spring.

## Calathea (kal-ath-e-a)

From the greek *kalathos*, basket, referring to the native use of the leaves in basket-weaving *(Marantaceae)*. These shade-loving, warm greenhouse peren-

4

nial plants, mainly from Brazil, are remarkable for their brilliantly marked leaves. They flourish in a warm, moist atmosphere and when used as house plants the pots should be plunged in large containers filled with moist peat, but a greenhouse atmosphere is what they really require.

**Species cultivated** *C. backemiana*, 9 inches, silver-grey with bright green blotches, tuberous roots. *C. insignis*, 6-18 inches, light green, purple beneath. *C. lindeniana*, 1 foot, dark green with emerald-green zone, maroon beneath. *C. ornata*, 18 inches, much taller in the wild, a variable plant, dark green with pink or cream lines, dark purple beneath. *C. picturata*, 15 inches, dark green, silvery zone, maroon beneath. *C. veitchiana*, 2½ feet, blended shades of green. *C. zebrina*, 1½ feet, dark green with darker stripes, purple and greenish purple beneath.

**Cultivation** Pot moderately firmly in March in a compost of equal parts of coarse lumps of loam, peat, leafmould and silver sand. Maintain a winter temperature of 65–70 F (18-21 C). Water freely in summer, moderately at other times. Stand the pots on good drainage in a shady position. Propagation is by division in March.

## Chlorophytum (klor-o-fi-tum)

From the Greek *chloros*, green, *phyton*, a plant *(Liliaceae)*. Greenhouse plants with long narrow leaves, some with variegated leaves. They are interesting in that they produce long drooping flower stems ending in a tuft of leaves, forming an offset. These offsets may be detached and rooted for propagation purposes.

**Species cultivated** *C. comosum (syn. C. sternbergianum)*, 1–2 feet, white flowers in summer. *C. elatum* (syns. *C. anthericum, C. capense* and *Phalangium elatum*), 1–1½ feet, white flowers in summer; var. *variegatum* has creamy white longitudinal variegations on the leaves.

**Cultivation** Grow the variegated and tall kinds in pots in a compost composed of equal parts of loam, leafmould, peat and sand. The drooping kinds should be grown in baskets or pots suspended in a greenhouse or window. Plants can be used for bedding out of doors from June to September. Pot up the young plants in March, and from March to October keep them at temperatures of 55–65 F (13–18 C), for the remainder of the year

**4 Calathae ornata**, a showy plant introduced from Columbia in 1849 of which there are now innumerable very popular forms.
**5 Chlorophytum elatum variegatum** which is frequently grown for its white-striped foliage. These stripes are devoid of chlorophyll.
**6 Chorizema ilicifolium**, a prostrate shrub from Western Australia which flowers in summer and is happy trailing up and down wires or walls.

at 45–50 F (7–10 C). Water freely during the summer but only moderately during winter. Propagate by seeds sown $\frac{1}{8}$ inch deep in pots containing well-drained light soil at a temperature of 65 F (18 C) in March, by offshoots taken in April and placed singly in pots under a bell jar put in a window or greenhouse, or by division of roots when repotting.

## Chorizema (kor-e-zee-ma)
From the Greek *choros,* a dance, *zema,* a drink; the name is said to have been given to the plant by the French explorer, J. J. H. de Labillardière, in Australia, on finding fresh water *(Leguminosae)*. A genus of evergreen shrubs and sub-shrubs, consisting of about 20 species, all from Australia. They used to be most popular plants in Edwardian conservatories, but they are less grown today. They are trailing plants which can be led up (or down) wires and trellises or the wall of a greenhouse, or over a wire frame.

**Species cultivated** *C. cordatum,* 10 feet, yellow and red flowers, April; vars. *elatior,* red flowers, *flavum,* orange-yellow. *C. diversifolium,* 2 feet, orange-red flowers, May. *C. ilicifolium,* 2–3 feet, yellow flowers, summer. *C. varium* (syn. *C. chandleri*), 4 feet, yellow and red flowers, May.

## Cineraria (sin-er-air-e-a)
From the Latin *cinereus,* ash-coloured, referring to the colour of the undersides of the leaves. All but a very few species (none of which are likely to be found in cultivation) have been transferred to the genus *Senecio.*

**Florist's cinerarias** The florist's cinerarias, obtainable in a very wide range of beautiful colours, have been derived from *Senecio cruentus* (once known as *Cineraria cruenta*), a herbaceous perennial from the Canary Islands. Although the plants are strictly perennials they are almost invariably grown as half-hardy annuals or biennials, for greenhouse display or for spring window boxes. Seed is obtainable of various strains in mixed colours, under such names as *hybrida grandiflora,* producing plants about 18–24 inches tall; 'Berlin Market', not quite so tall, in various rich shades; 'Hansa Strain', 18 inches, bright colours, compact plants; 'Rainbow', 18 inches, pinks and pale blues; 'Cremer's Prize', 18 inches, medium-sized flowers, freely produced; *stellata,* $2\frac{1}{2}$ feet, large heads of small, star-shaped flowers in very varied colours; *multiflora nana,* 1 foot, dwarf plants, self-coloured flowers. In addition there are certain named colour cultivars growing to about 21 inches tall, including *atroviolacea,* large dark violet flowers; 'Matador', coppery scarlet; *sanguinea,* blood-red.

**Cultivation** To produce winter-flowering plants seed should be sown in April or early May in the heated greenhouse, in

a temperature of 55–60°F (13–16°C). Seed for spring-flowering plants should be sown in an unheated frame in June or early July. Sow thinly in John Innes seed compost, covering the seed only lightly. When the seedlings have developed three leaves pot them up into deep seed boxes. Give them plenty of light and air; pot them on again singly into 3 inch pots before they become crowded, then into 6 inch pots when the 3 inch pots are filled with roots. Large, vigorous plants may need a further potting into 7 or 8 inch pots; this should be done by the end of October. John Innes potting composts are perfectly suitable. Once they have been potted singly the plants should be moved out into the cold frame and kept shaded. They may remain there until about mid-October, given plenty of ventilation, both by day and by night. They will still need ample ventilation

after they have been brought into the greenhouse where they should be placed on the staging as near to the glass as possible. Feed the plants with weak liquid manure or fertiliser, twice weekly from September onwards and spray them against attacks by aphids and leaf miners. From late October until the plants have finished flowering and are either discarded or used to provide cuttings, the temperature in the greenhouse should be 45–50°F (7–10°C). However, cuttings are hardly ever used to propagate these plants, unless it is to increase a specially desirable variety.

## Citrus (sit-rus)
From the Greek *kitron,* citron, *(Rutaceae)*. A small genus of evergreen shrubs and trees usually more or less spiny. They include the oranges, lemons, grapefruit, lime and other citrus fruits.

*C. mitis*, the calamondin or Panama orange, small tree, small white flowers, becoming increasingly popular as a decorative pot plant, fruiting when quite small, Phillipines. *C. nobilis*, the king orange, 15 feet, flower buds tinged red, white within, China; var. *deliciosa*, mandarine, tangerine. *C. sinensis*, the sweet orange, 20–30 feet, white flowers, Asia; the Navel orange is a variety. *C. taitensis*, the otaheite orange, fragrant flowers pink outside, sometimes grown as a pot plant, origin unknown. **Cultivation** Plants grown for their fruit need a lofty, well-lighted, cool house where the winter temperature can be held at 40–50°F (4–10°C). Growth is made early in the year and if the plants need repotting this must be done after the main growth has been made. The plants can be grown in borders with good drainage or in well-drained tubs or large pots, in a fairly heavy loam plus well-rotted manure. It is advisable to syringe with water daily during the summer and the roots must never be allowed to dry out. Weak shoots should be pruned out during the summer, dead wood removed and branches thinned, if need be, during winter.

Seedling citrus plants make good house plants. *C. limonia* and *C. taitensis* are suitable compact species. They should be grown in an ordinary potting compost and put out of doors in summer to harden the wood. Propagation is by seed sown ½ inch deep in light soil in March at a temperature of 55°F (13°C). These seedlings produce stocks on which selected choice varieties can be grafted the following March. Cuttings inserted in small pots of sandy soil in July, will root readily; shoots may also be layered in October or plants may be budded in August.

## Coleus (ko-le-us)
From the Greek, *koleos*, a sheath, referring to the combined stamens (*Labiateae*). Warm greenhouse plants from the tropics, of which one, *C. blumei*, is grown mainly for its highly ornamental nettle-like foliage; variegated, self-coloured and often brilliantly edged. Colours include green, purple, bronze, white, scarlet, pink and yellow.

They can be grown as fruiting plants in the heated greenhouse; some make decorative room plants.
**Species cultivated** *C. aurantifolia,* the lime, 8–15 feet, small white flowers, tropical Asia; the young growth is very sensitive to frost. *C. aurantium,* the Seville or bitter orange, 20–30 feet, white flowers, tropical Asia, the hardiest of the genus; vars. *melitensis,* the blood orange; *myrtifolia,* spineless. *C. bergamia,* the bergamot orange, small tree, small, very sweet-smelling white flowers, the skin yields an essential oil used in the manufacture of Eau de Cologne, Calabriā. *C. japonica,* see *Fortunella japonica. C. limonia,* the lemon, 8–10 feet, flowers tinged red in bud, white when open; there are several varieties differing in size of fruit, Asia. *C. maxima* and *C. paradisi,* 15–18 feet are similar. They are the grapefruits, or shaddocks, with large white flowers, young specimens are sensitive to frost but sensitivity decreases with age, Polynesia, Eastern Asia. *C. medica,* the citron, 8–10 feet, flower buds reddish, flowers white inside, skin the basis of candied peel, Asia; var. *sarcodactylis* is Etrog, the Jewish sacred citron.

**Cineraria hybrida grandiflora (opposite page) is typical of modern strains of this wide-ranging plant. The name comes from the Latin word cinereus, meaning ash-coloured, which refers to the shades to be seen on the underside of the plant. The seeds should be sown in April or early May in a heated greenhouse at a temperature of 13-16°C. The temperature should be approximately 5°C lower during flowering, which should start in October. Citrus mitis (this page), the Panama Orange, is becoming increasingly popular as a decorative pot-plant as it fruits when small.**

**1** Species cultivated *C. blumei*, 1–1½ feet perennial, giving rise to the many brilliant colour variations. *C. frederici*, to 4 feet, annual or biennial, deep blue flowers, December. *C. thyrsoideus*, 3 feet, perennial, bright blue flowers, winter.

**Cultivation** Use John Innes potting compost in 5–6 inch pots. Keep adequately warm and moist. Summer temperatures, 60–65°F (16–18°C), winter, 55°F (13°C), minimum, 45°F (7°C). Water well during the warm season, less so during the cooler months. Ventilate when temperatures exceed the summer optimum. Weak liquid feeding is beneficial throughout summer. Shade only when essential. Higher temperatures are required for the winter flowerers, especially during winter, 50–60°F (10–16°C). Propagation is by seed sown February, March and April, barely covered in a temperature of 70°F (21°C), or by cuttings of young shoots taken at almost any time and rooted in a propagating frame with bottom heat. Stop young plants by pinching out the growing point to induce bushiness. Strike cuttings of winter flowerers from April to June. Named coleus with decorative foliage, which can be raised from seed include: 'Autumn Splendour', buff-brown with green edge; 'Candidus', green and ivory; 'Red Velvet'; 'Rembrandt', wine, scarlet and bronze.

## Cryptanthus (krip-tan-thus)

From the Greek *kryptos*, hidden, *anthos*, flower, the flowers being concealed by the bracts *(Bromeliaceae)*. Sometimes called 'earth stars' an allusion to their starfish-like shapes. A small genus of dwarf, tufted, spiny plants from Brazil, suitable for the stovehouse or as house plants. The flowers are mostly white, and borne in a dense tuft of bracts in the centre of the rosette. Mostly they flower in summer. As house plants they are grown for their handsome foliage.

**Species cultivated** *C. acaulis*, 6 inches, green leaves, white flowers, some varieties with variegated leaves. *C. beuckeri*, 6 inches, leaves mottled green and cream, flowers white and red. *C. bivittatus*, 8 inches, leaves banded with buff above, brown below, flowers white; vars. *major*, larger in all its parts; *roseo-pictus*, leaves flushed pink with cream stripes. *C. fosterianus*, 12 inches, leaves green, red and grey, banded brown. *C. lacerdae*, 6 inches, leaves emerald green, margined and striped silvery grey, flowers white. *C.* × *osyanus*, leaves brownish red, mottled pink and red, white flowers, hybrid. *C. tricolor*, 10 inches, leaves cream, striped green, flushed pink. *C. unicolor*, 6 inches, pale pink leaves. *C.*

There are many forms of Coleus blumei, all grown for the brilliantly coloured leaves. 2 Coleus thyrosideus was introduced from Central Africa in 1897. It produces its tall spikes of blue flowers in winter

*zonatus*, 6–9 inches, leaves banded green and grey, flowers white; vars. *argyraeus*, leaves banded green and golden-brown; *zebrinus*, leaves banded grey and maroon.

**Cultivation** Pot these plants in March in equal parts of loam, rough peat, leaf-mould and silver sand. Plenty of water and good drainage is needed. Temperatures: September to March 65–75°F (18–24°C), March to September 75–85°F (24–29 C). Stolons are produced in the outer leaf axils, making offsets which can be removed for propagation. When grown as house plants they should be kept dry or nearly dry in winter. In the house they need a light position; the smaller kinds are suitable for growing in bottle gardens.

### Cyclamen (sik-la-men)
From the Greek *kyklos*, a circle, referring to the coiling of the flower stems of some species after flowering *(Primulaceae)*. Sowbread. A valuable genus of dwarf tuberous plants, natives of the Mediterranean area, some flowering in autumn and early spring out of doors, others in the greenhouse or conservatory for winter decoration. Showy, neat and

**1 Cyclamen are deservedly popular as pot plants for winter and spring decoration. Easily raised from seed sown under glass, high temperatures are not required. 2 This group shows the sturdy growth and the wide variety in colour. 3 The modern strains produce large, elegant blooms on strong stems. 4 The 'Salmon Pink' strain**

easy to cultivate, they belong to the same family as the primrose. Most species are on the borderline of hardiness in the British Isles, and whereas some flourish happily in sheltered gardens, the beauty of others may be best appreciated in an alpine house or cold greenhouse, or a sheltered sink garden or scree frame. In many species the flower stalk twists like a spring after the flowers have faded, to draw the seed capsules down to ground level.

For alpine house or cold greenhouse cultivation plant the tubers of hardy species in summer for the autumn-flowering kinds and in late September or October for the winter and spring-flowering species, in a compost of 2 parts of loam to 1 part of leafmould and sand, and let the snout of the tuber show above the soil level. Cover the

compost with limestone chippings to ensure surface drainage. Water as required up to and during flowering time, gradually reducing watering after flowering. Plunge the pots in peat or ashes out of doors during the summer months to

51

make room in the greenhouse and to rest the tubers. Repot, start to water and return to the greenhouse in September. Propagation is from seed sown in pans in the autumn in a temperature of 45–55°F (7–13°C), but germination is often slow. The small plants are pricked off and potted up singly once the tubers swell.

**Cultivation of Cyclamen persicum** A cold greenhouse or living room window-sill is suitable for *C. persicum*, when cultivation is as described for cold greenhouse sorts. These plants are extensively forced for winter decoration and have come to be known as florists' cyclamen. In August soak the pot and tuber that have previously been dried off all summer and once the tiny leaves begin to sprout, repot in a fresh compost of 2 parts of loam to 1 part of leafmould and sand. The tuber should be potted so that the level of the soil surrounds its circumference, no deeper. Keep close for a few days until growth starts again. Syringe daily, keep the plants shaded and maintain a moist atmosphere and temperature of 55–60°F (13–16°C). Water moderately and feed weekly with a liquid feed throughout the flowering period which, with a selection of plants, can be from November to March. Remove old blossoms and leaves by tugging them out from the base of the stem. After flowering, gradually dry off, resting the tubers out of doors in a dry frame or plunge bed during the summer months. Propagation is from seed sown in very fine compost between mid-August and mid-November in a temperature of 50–60°F (10–16°C). Prick off the seedlings and then pot them into thumb pots. Subsequently pot them on, with the necks of the tubers well above soil level. In August gentle forcing can begin. One-year old plants give the finest flowers, though tubers can be grown on from year to year, but it is advisable to raise a fresh supply of plants each autumn for good results the following winter.

Numerous strains have been produced, many of which come true from seed. Seed of mixed colours is usually sown and the resultant range of colour is very wide. Strains of self colour can be purchased under such names as 'Bonfire', scarlet; 'Mauve Queen', purple-mauve; 'Pink Pearl', deep salmon pink; 'Salmon King', pale salmon pink.

## Cyperus (si-per-us)

From the Greek *kypeiros*, a sedge (*Cyperaceae*). Greenhouse and hardy perennials belonging to the sedge family, grown for their foliage. The long, narrow, grass-like leaves are produced at the tops of the slender stems and radiate like the ribs of an umbrella, hence the common name of umbrella plant given to *C. alternifolius,* a good house plant in moderately warm rooms.
**Species cultivated Greenhouse** *C. alter-*

*nifolius,* umbrella plant, 2½ feet, spikelets brown; vars. *variegatus,* leaves striped white; *gracilis,* 1 foot, an elegant form with narrower leaves, *C. diffusus,* 2–3 feet, very long leaves, spikelets greenish to brown; var. *variegatus,* leaves variegated white. *C. papyrus* (syn. *Papyrus antiquorum*), Egyptian paper reed, papyrus, 8–10 feet, good dark green.
**Hardy** *C. esculentus,* chufa, 2–3 feet, producing edible underground tubers known as tiger nuts in southern Europe. *C. longus,* 4 feet, a good foliage foil for poolside planting.
**Cultivation** The plants are semi-aquatic in nature and require quantities of water, which is best given by standing the pots in a shallow vessel of water. A compost of equal parts of loam and leafmould maintains the moisture well. *C. alternifolius* can be divided each March and repotted to maintain a supply of young plants. Out of doors the plants lend themselves to planting in boggy situations and on the margins of pools. Plant either in autumn or

spring, preferably spring, and remove the dead stems when faded, otherwise the plant has a very untidy appearance.

## Dasylirion (das-ee-lir-e-on)

From the Greek *dasys,* thick, *lirion,* a lily, referring to the succulent leaves (*Liliaceae*). Greenhouse evergreen foliage plants, related to the yuccas. The leaves grow in a tuft from the short stem and are narrow, several feet in length, tough, leathery and with spines along the margins. They grow

upright for more than 1½ feet, then the tops curve outwards. The small flowers are bell shaped.
**Species cultivated** *D. acrotriche,* 6–8 feet, flowers white. *D. glaucophyllum,* 10 feet, white. *D. hookeri,* 3 feet, purplish. *D. serratifolium,* 2 feet, white. All from Mexico.

**Cultivation** These plants are almost hardy and the pots in which they are grown may be put out of doors in the summer, particularly for creating sub-tropical bedding effects, or they may be

used as conservatory or house plants all the year round. Water is needed frequently during the summer but little should be given from October to March. Pot very firmly in February or March, in a compost of 2 parts of loam and peat to 1 part of sand. Maintain a minimum winter temperature of 45°F (7°C). Propagation is by seed sown in March in a cold frame or greenhouse.

## Dieffenbachia (dee-fen-bak-e-a)

Commemorating J. F. Dieffenbach, early nineteenth century German physician and botanist *(Araceae)*. Dumb cane. Tender evergreen perennials from tropical America, grown for their foliage and used for greenhouse and room decoration. The large oval leaves spread outwards and downwards from the central stem and are spotted or lined with white or cream. The plants are poisonous in all their parts and are said to have been fed to slaves to render them dumb for several days.

**Species cultivated** *D. amoena*, laeves 1–2 feet long, 6–10 inches wide, heavily marked with cream. *D. bowmannii*, leaves to 2½ feet long, 1 foot wide (smaller when grown as a house plant), mottled with dark and light green. *D. imperialis*, leaves 1–2 feet long, 3–4 inches wide, blotched with cream. *D. oerstedii*, leaves 9–10 inches long, 4½ inches wide, dark green with ivory-striped mid-rib. *D. picta*, leaves 9 inches long, 3 inches wide, heavily marked with cream, but very variable in size and markings; vars. *bausei*, leaves bright green, blotched and spotted with dark green and silver (possibly a hybrid); *jenmanii*, leaves narrower; *memoria*, leaves silvery-grey, margins dark green; *roehrsii*, leaves wider, pale yellow-green, dark green midrib and margins, ivory veins.

**Cultivation** A rich compost of equal parts of peat, loam and a quarter part of sand and well-rotted manure is needed. Pot in February or March and water freely until September, then water moderately only during the winter. Syringe daily during the height of summer and shade from strong sun. Indoors the plants should not be kept in a bright window. A winter temperature of not less than 50–55°F (10–13°C) is needed. Propagation is by stem cuttings 1–2 inches long taken in spring or summer and inserted in sandy compost in a propagating case. There is a tendency to drop the lower leaves and if the top is treated as a stem cutting in a propagating case roots will soon be formed.

1 Dasylirion acrotriche growing out of doors in the warmth of Tresco.
2 Cyperus alternifolius, a good house plant for a moderately warm room.
3 Dieffenbachia picta, a poisonous plant, is best grown in a warm greenhouse.
4 The attractive Dracaena victoriae.

## Dracaena (dras-ee-na)

From the Greek *drakaina,* a female dragon; *D. draco,* the dragon tree, yields the colouring matter known as dragon's blood *(Liliaceae).* Evergreen plants from the tropics grown in warm greenhouses for the handsome, often variegated, foliage. They are related to *Cordyline* and often confused with that genus. The flowers of dracaena are usually larger and the rootstock is not creeping as in *Cordyline.*

**Species cultivated** *D. concinna,* 6 feet, leaves green with red margin, Mauritius. *D. draco,* dragon tree, 40–60 feet, leaves glaucous, Canary Isles, where there is an aged, world-famous specimen over 70 feet high. Hardy in the Isles of Scilly and parts of Cornwall. Young plants are decorative under glass. *D. fragrans,* up to 20 feet, glossy green, recurved leaves, yellow flowers in clusters, fragrant, Guinea. *D. godseffiana,* 3 feet, leaves green with cream spots, flowers yellowish or red, Congo. *D. goldieana,* 4–6 feet, leaves glossy yellowish-green, marked silver-green, tropical West Africa. *D. sanderiana,* 5 feet, leaves green with a broad white margin, Congo.

**Cultivation** Pot in February or March in a compost of 2 parts of loam, 1 part of peat and 1 part of leafmould and sharp sand. Stand in a light position. The minimum winter temperature should be about 60°F (16°C). Water moderately in winter, freely during the spring and summer. Propagation is by seed sown in March in sandy soil in a temperature of 85°F (29°C). Cuttings may be made in March or April from the main stem, cut into 2 inch lengths and partially buried horizontally in sandy peat. Or the plants may be propagated by pieces of the fleshy root placed in sandy peat in spring, or by the tops of stems placed in sand in March or April.

## Echeveria (ek-ev-eer-e-a)

Commemorating Atanasio Echeverria, Mexican botanical artist *(Crassulaceae).* Greenhouse and half-hardy, low-growing succulent plants, formerly included in *Cotyledon;* mostly of upright growth with large fleshy leaves in rosettes, many well coloured and waxy in appearance.

**Species cultivated** *E. agavoides,* very thick fleshy leaves, long and pointed, flowers red and carmine, central Mexico. *E. bella,* forms clumps, flowers orange-yellow, Mexico. *E. gibbiflora,* stems strong, erect, leaves broad and shiny, flowers light red with yellow centre, Mexico; vars. *caruncula,* with raised rough parts to the centre of leaf; *metallica,* leaves bronze edged with red. *E. harmsii* (syns. *E. elegans, Oliveranthus elegans*), much branched shrubby plant, 1–1½ feet tall, each branch ending in a rosette of leaves, large flowers, 1 inch long, red, tipped yellow, a most handsome species, Mexico.

**Cultivation** The compost should be made from John Innes potting compost No. 1, with a sixth part added of grit, sand and broken brick. Pot the plants in March and place them in a sunny position. Old plants get very leggy and lose their lower leaves. The tops can then be cut off and rooted and the old stem will send out fresh shoots. Water from April to September, but give none in winter unless the plants are in a warm room when they should be watered once a month. They may be planted out of doors in early June and removed to the greenhouse in September. Some, particularly *E. gibbiflora metallica,* are used in summer bedding schemes as edging plants. Propagation is by seed sown in John Innes seed compost at a temperature of 70°F (21°C), in early spring. Shade the seedlings from strong sunshine, prick them out when large enough. Plants are also readily increased from cuttings, including leaves. It is also possible to flower young shoots. Flower scapes cut off and dried can make roots.

## Erythrina (er-ith-ri-na)

From the Greek *erythros,* red, the colour of the flowers *(Leguminosae).* A small genus of tender deciduous shrubs and half-hardy perennials.

**Species cultivated** *E. crista-galli,* coral

1 Echeveria elegans makes an attractive pot plant for the home.
2 Dracaena (Cordyline) terminalis, a stove house plant grown for its ornamental foliage.

tree, shrub to 6–8 feet, flowers bright scarlet in bold spikes on the ends of shoots, leaves leathery, somewhat glaucous, stems prickly, June to August, Brazil; var. *compacta*, less tall, more compact in habit. *E. herbacea*, 2–3 feet, herbaceous plant, flowers deep scarlet, borne in long spikes, June to September, West Indies.

**Cultivation** The coral tree can only be grown in the open in the most sheltered gardens. Otherwise it should be grown in the warm greenhouse, in a large pot or tub containing equal parts of loam, peat, old manure and sharp sand. Repot when necessary in March. Water freely from April to September. Stand the container in the open during the summer. Cut the plant hard back in October, and keep it almost dry during the winter in a frost-free shed or greenhouse. This applies to both shrubby and herbaceous species. Propagation of shrubby species is by cuttings in the spring, removed with a piece of old wood attached and inserted singly in pots containing sandy peat in a propagating frame, with a temperature of 75°C (24°C). Herbaceous species may be divided in spring.

## Euphorbia (u-for-be-a)

Named after Euphorbus, physician to King Juba of Mauritania *(Euphorbiaceae)*. A genus of about a thousand species, widely distributed, mainly in temperate regions, showing immense diversity of form and requirements. They include annual, biennial and perennial herbaceous plants, shrubs and trees and succulent plants. The decorative parts are really bracts, often colourful, round the small and inconspicuous flowers. Some are warm greenhouse plants others are hardy. The succulent species are mainly from Africa, most of them from South and West Africa. Many of those resemble cacti in appearance. All euphorbias exude a poisonous milky latex when the stems are cut and this can often burn the skin and the eyes and which, in some species, is poisonous if taken internally.

**Greenhouse species cultivated** (non-succulent), *E. fulgens* (syn. *E. jacquinaeflora*), 2–3 feet, small leafy shrub, scarlet bracts carried on the upper side of young shoots, autumn and winter, Mexico. *E. pulcherrima* (syn. *Poinsettia pulcherrima*), poinsettia, 3–6 feet, brilliant scarlet showy bracts in winter, Mexico. The modern Ecke hybrids are increasing in popularity. They include 'Barbara Ecke', fluorescent carmine bracts; 'Pink Ecke', coral pink and 'White Ecke', white. Some have variegated foliage. Even more popular

**1 Erythrina crista-galli compacta, a more compact form of the coral tree. The flowers appear from June to August.**
**2 Mikkelsen Pink, a popular new strain of Euphorbia pulcherrima.**

now is the Mikkelsen strain, introduced in 1964. These, with shorter stems and with bracts in scarlet, pink or white, are a good deal 'hardier' in that they will withstand lower temperatures and fluctuating temperatures, yet will retain their bracts and remain colourful for 5–6 weeks.

**Cultivation** Greenhouse, non-succulent species: a good compost is 4 parts of fibrous loam, 1 part of decayed cow manure and a half part of silver sand. Young plants should be potted into 6- or 8-inch pots in summer and kept in a cold house or frame until September. Then feed regularly with a liquid feed and bring into a temperature of 60–65 F (16–18 C) to bring the plants into flower in December. After flowering, reduce watering and temperature until the soil is quite dry. In April cut back to two buds and start to water. Repot in May when the young shoots are about 1 inch long. Pot on as required; in high summer the pots can be stood out of doors or kept in a cold frame and brought in again in September. Propagation is from cuttings of young shoots taken in summer and inserted in sand in a temperature of 70 F (21 C).

## Fatshedera (fats-hed-er-a)

A compound name from *Fatsia* and *Hedera*, the two genera involved *(Araliaceae)*. A bi-generic hybrid between *Fatsia japonica* and an ivy, possibly *Hedera helix*. The deep green leaves are leathery and glossy and palmate, shaped like a five-pointed star. It originated in France in 1911, and nowadays is a popular house plant. There is but one species, × *F. lizei*, which makes erect, rather wiry growth on a single stem which needs support. The leaves are carried all round the stem. *F. l. variegata* is a variegated form with a broad cream margin to each leaf, otherwise of similar habit. The plants sometimes flower in autumn but are grown for their decorative foliage.

**Cultivation** Both plants are hardy and can be grown out of doors; the variegated form is a little less happy in such circumstances, but normally they are used as house plants. Tolerant of most conditions and treatment, they are easy to manage provided that they are kept moist and in semi-shade during the growing season. The variegated form tends to drop its leaves in poor light and in a dry warm room during winter. Repot in spring or early summer when the plant gets too big for its pot, using John Innes potting compost. Propagation is easily effected by stem cuttings.

**1 The Poinsettia, the most common and certainly one of the most attractive of the many offspring of Euphorbia.**
**2 Fatshedera lizei variegata has cream margins to its decorative leaves.**
**3 Fatsia japonica has ball-like heads of creamy flowers in autumn.**

**Fatsia** (fat-se-a)

From the Japanese *fatsi*, the name for *F. japonica (Araliaceae)*. A genus of two species of evergreen, slightly tender shrubs, related to *Aralia*, with large and striking leaves like a seven-pointed star. There are but two species, of which the only one likely to be found in cultivation is *F. japonica* (syns. *Aralia sieboldii* and *Aralia japonica*), rice paper plant, fig-leaf palm, false castor-oil plant, a native of Japan, 6–15 feet tall, with dark shining leaves which branch out on long stalks from the main stem, and are quite often up to a foot or more across. The variety *variegata* has white tips to the leaf lobes. Both bear many-branched heads of milk-white flowers in rounded clusters in October and November, followed by black fruits.

**Cultivation** *Fatsia japonica*, a useful late-flowering evergreen, can be grown out of doors in a partially shaded position, protected from wind. Plant out in May, allowing sufficient room as it is a strong-growing plant. It makes a good house plant when young, particularly in spacious surroundings; it is ideal for public buildings and spacious conservatories. Pot up in the spring in a compost of 2 parts of sandy loam, 1 part of leaf-mould, sand and old dry manure; water regularly during the summer months but moderately only from September to March. It should be kept just free from frost, though, when grown out of doors, it will stand a good many degrees of frost without severe injury.

**Ficus** (fi-kus or fee-kus)

The Latin name for a fig tree, possibly derived from the Hebrew name *fag (Moraceae)*. Fig. A large genus of both evergreen and deciduous trees and shrubby climbing plants, widely distributed over the warmer parts of the world. All have monoecious (unisexual) flowers. In ficus both male and female flowers are contained within a receptacle which later ripens into a fruit. The most common in this country is the fruiting fig, other species can most commonly be found as house plants and maybe in conservatory decoration. They vary enormously in size and shape of leaf, and in form, some climbing, others clinging, but all emitting a milky sap or latex when cut. All except the fig tree are treated as tender in this country, although *F. pumila* is only slightly tender and is sometimes seen out of doors in the milder counties.

**Species cultivated** *F. australis* (syn. *F. rubiginosa*), shrub or small tree, leaves roundish about 3 inches across, brown underneath; var. *variegata*, a slow-growing variegated form. *F. benghalensis*, banyan tree, a native of Bengal where it attains 30 feet, has wiry aerial

**Ficus elastica variegata, the India-rubber Plant, a good room plant, is also valuable for greenhouse decoration.**

with dark green, leathery, glossy leaves, 6–12 inches long, growing in steps around a central stem; vars. *decora*, a better form with larger leaves held slightly upright, with red under-surfaces and red leaf sheaths; *doescheri*, pale green with cream markings and near white margins. pale pink leaf sheaths. *F. lyrata* (syn. *F. pandurata*), fiddle-back fig, large, 'waisted', leathery leaves, generally with the silhouette of a violin. *F. macrophylla*, Moreton Bay fig, similar to *F. elastica decora*, but leaves narrower, with pale green sheaths. *F. parcellii*, a lovely Polynesian species that needs the warm, moist conditions of a stovehouse, leaves variegated white and green, fruits striped. *F. pumila* (syn. *F. repens*), a rapid climber or creeper with small heart-shaped leaves, the branches bearing tiny 'suckers' (aerial roots, similar to those of ivy) by which it attaches itself to a support. It can also be grown as a trailing plant; var. *minima*, more slender is used in hanging baskets. *F. radicans*, creeping, leaves larger than in *F. pumila*; var. *variegata*, cream variegated.

**Cultivation** A compost of 2 parts of sandy loam to 1 part of peat, or John Innes potting compost No. 2 or 3, is suitable and the plants should always be in a pot that seems to be a size too small for them. A minimum winter temperature of 50 F (10 C) is necessary. Pot up or repot in autumn or spring and water freely when growing, but in winter allow the plants to dry out completely between watering. The main demerit of ficus plants is that they drop their lower leaves (even more so after overwatering) but a leggy plant can be rescued by 'ringing' the stem, by slitting it below the leaves, packing damp moss around it and binding this with polythene, making sure to give support to the weakened stem. Roots form at this point and will soon penetrate the moss. When they have developed sufficiently the top of the plant can be severed and potted up separately. The remainder of the plant will produce leaves and growths again from the base if it is cut back.

Sponge the leaves regularly with soft water and syringe daily in spring and summer when grown under glass.

Propagation is by cuttings made about 6 inches long, or from eyes taken as for vine eyes and inserted in a sandy compost in heat, at least 60–65 F (16–18 C) in spring.

1 Fittonia argyroneura is a dwarf trailing plant with white-veined leaves, popular in warm greenhouses.
2 Ficus benjamina and Ficus radicans variegata are both excellent house plants for conservatories and decoration.

roots hanging in bunches from the lower leaf nodes, leaves dark green, leathery, 4–9 inches long, covered with a brown down when young, can be restricted to house plant dimensions. *F. benjamina*, of birch tree form, graceful and weeping with ovate, glossy, apple-green leaves. *F. carica*, common fig, 15 feet or more, deeply five-lobed leaves, the middle lobe largest, bright, dark green, fruits edible, varying in shape and colour. *F. diversifolia* (syn. *F. deltoides*), mistletoe fig, dark matt green, leathery leaves, small orange fruits. *F. elastica*, India rubber plant, the most popularly grown species

## Fittonia (fit-o-ne-a)
Named for Elizabeth and Sarah Mary Fitton, nineteenth century botanists *(Acanthaceae)*. Evergreen trailing plants from Peru, for the warm greenhouse, grown mainly for their oval, brightly coloured leaves.

**Species cultivated** *F. argyroneura*, dwarf trailing plant, white-veined leaves. *F. gigantes*, 12–15 inches, leaves green, veined with red. *F. verschaffeltii*, 8

inches, green leaves, veins red; var. *pearcei*, leaves veined with carmine red. **Cultivation** These plants need a greenhouse with a minimum winter temperature of 55°F (13°C). Grow them preferably in shallow pans or in the border of the house, always in a shaded position. The compost should be of equal proportions of sand, loam and peat and plants should be put in about 3 inches apart. A considerable amount of water is needed in summer and daily syringeing to produce a moist atmosphere is beneficial. They are occasionally grown as house plants, but it is usually difficult to provide the moist atmosphere they like, other than in a bottle garden or similar container. Propagation is from cuttings of young shoots in February, March or April, inserted in sand in a propagating case. Alternatively the plants can be divided in early spring, and repotted separately.

## Fuchsia (fu-sha)

Commemorating Leonard Fuchs, sixteenth-century German botanical writer and professor of medicine *(Onagraceae)*. A genus of about 100 species of shrubs mostly for the greenhouse, a few hardy. Most of the fuchsias grown today are hybrids, of which thousands have been raised in the past 120 years or so, and more and more make their appearance each year. A typical fuchsia flower consists of the tube and sepals, usually of one colour, the petals (corolla), usually differing in colour from the tube and sepals (if the colours are the same, the variety is known as a self-coloured variety) and the protruding stamens and style. When describing the colours of fuchsia flowers it is conventional to give that of the tube and sepals (t and s) first, followed by that of the corolla (c). Double and single flowered varieties are available and the modern trend is to produce larger flowered varieties.

**Hardy species cultivated** Some of these may be killed to the ground in cold weather but produce new growth again in spring. *F. excorticata*, tree to 40 feet in its native habitat, a tall shrub in the milder counties of Great Britain, elsewhere a low bush, not reliably hardy, flowers 1 inch long, calyx yellow, sepals violet and green, New Zealand. *F. exoniensis*, 6 feet, resembles *F. magellanica*, one of its parents, but with larger flowers, hybrid. *F. magellanica* (syn. *F. macrostemma*), 6–20 feet, the scarlet and purple flowered 'typical' fuchsia, graceful in growth; vars. *alba*, pale pink; *gracilis* (syn. *F. gracilis*), more slender; *g. variegata*, leaves silver, pink and rose; *riccartonii*, scarlet and violet purple, used as a hedge plant in mild localities; *versicolor*, leaves grey-green and slightly variegated, South America. *F. parviflora*, prostrate, calyx crimson, petals coral-red, Mexico, hardy in mildest areas. *F. reflexa*, similar to *F. parviflora*, flowers cerise.

**Hardy cultivars** 'Caledonia', reddish cerise and reddish violet, free-flowering, lax habit; 'Chilleton Beauty', white edged pink and violet-mauve, vigorous habit; 'Corallina', scarlet and reddish-purple, vigorous, lax habit; 'Dunrobin Bedder', scarlet and purple, dwarf; 'Madam Cornelissen', crimson and white, semi-double; 'Mrs Popple', scarlet and purple, free-flowering; 'Mrs W. P. Wood', pink and white, free-flowering; 'Tom Thumb', cerise and mauve, dwarf; 'Tresco', scarlet and deep purple.

**Cultivation** These hardy or near hardy kinds need a deep rich soil and a well-drained position. Plant in autumn or spring and cut back old growth in February close to the base of the plant. They may require some protection in winter in the form of ashes or peat litter. Propagation is from seed or cuttings as for the tender types.

**Greenhouse species** Only the connoisseur and collector grows the species as they are far superseded by the named varieties, but several species are worth cultivating. *F. corymbiflora*, 4–6 feet, long, deep red flowers, Peru. *F. fulgens*, 3–4 feet, long coral scarlet flowers, Mexico. *F. procumbens*, trailing, calyx orange-yellow, sepals violet and green, stamens red and blue, fruits large and red, New Zealand; can be grown out of doors in very mild districts. *F. serratifolia*, 6–8 feet, pink, scarlet and

**Opposite page: Fuchsia 'Corallina', a vigorous example of the attractive Fuchsia family.**
**This page: Fuchsia 'Mrs Popple', a free-flowering hardy cultivar, has scarlet and purple flowers.**

Among the named cultivars the range of colour and flowering time is so wide that it is possible, by selection of variety and growing habits, to ensure a long display of flower. So many are available that it is possible to give a selection only here.

**Bush trained varieties** 'Burning Bush', pale yellowish-green foliage with red veins and stems, coral-magenta flowers; 'Beauty of Bath', semi-double pink, white and carmine flowers; 'Glitters', a single, waxy, orange-red; 'Mission Bells', cyclamen-pink and heliotrope, semi-double, calyx reflexed; 'Mrs Lovell Swisher', ivory and pink; 'Party Frock', rose tube, blue corolla and pink; 'Pink Favourite', rose-pink self; 'Swanley Gem', an old variety, single, violet and scarlet; 'Swingtime', rich red and white; 'Texas Longhorn', a giant flower, up to 8 inches across, not everyone's favourite, red and white; 'Topaz', light coral and violet; 'Vanessa', double, pale carmine and lilac.

**Cascade fuchsias** 'Angel's Flight', pink and white rather a long flower; 'Cara Mia', semi-double, shrimp-pink and white; 'Falling Stars', coral with blood-red tube; 'Fort Bragg', a recent introduction with double flowers of lilac with a rose tube; 'Golden Marinka', grown for its golden foliage, flowers deep red, semi-double; 'Marinka', semi-double, red, 'Red Ribbons', white with deep red spreading corolla; 'Red Spider', single crimson and deep rose, a tiny edging of crimson on the corolla.

**Standards** 'Angela Leslie', two tones of pink, double; 'Blue Lagoon', double flowers, very abundant, bright red tube, deep bluish-purple corolla; 'Bravado', large red and periwinkle-blue; 'Cascade', single, white and carmine; 'Citation', single, rose and white; 'Court Jester', red shrimp-pink and white; 'Pink Flamingo', pink and white; 'Pink Quartet', double, tube deep pink, corolla paler; 'Red Ribbons', red and white; 'Tennessee Waltz', rose and mauve.

**Fan training varieties** 'Curtain Call', carmine tube and sepals, deep rose corolla with darker flecks, double; 'Flirtation Waltz', white and pink, rather frilly corolla; 'Mission Bells', semi-double, violet and cyclamen; 'The Doctor', single, flesh-pink and orange-red.

**Cultivation** Fuchsias need a minimum winter temperature of 45–50 F (7–10 C) and can be used out of doors in summer as dot plants in bedding schemes, or for ribbon effects (varieties such as 'Tom Thumb'), to decorate loggias or as room plants. Window boxes look decorative when filled with such varieties as 'Benitchea', 'Evening Sky', 'Santa Lucia', 'Siena Blue', 'Tinker Bell', because they cascade slightly over the sides of the box.

Start plants into growth in February by syringeing daily and 'stop' them frequently during spring to encourage

## 3

**1** Fuchsias are noted for the width of both colour and flowering time. Fuchsia 'Sleigh Bells' is at one end of the colour spectrum.
**2** Fuchsia 'Beauty of Bath' has semi-double flowers in white and pink.
**3** Fuchsia 'Burning Bush' looks effective when planted on a patio in a large container. The pale, yellow-green foliage with red veins and stems is a good foil for the coral-magenta flowers.

green waxy flowers, winter, Peru. *F. simplicicaulis*, 12 feet, crimson flowers, autumn, Peru. *F. triphylla*, 1–1½ feet, cinnabar red flowers, West Indies. *F. triphylla* has given rise to a range of long-flowered, red-bronze-leaved hybrids, including 'Mantilla', carmine, and 'Thalia', a variety over a hundred years old with flame flowers and rich reddish foliage. Other species are listed by specialist growers.

bushiness or for training as required. Water moderately, feed once the flower buds show, remove seed pods to prolong the season and dry off somewhat after flowering in the sun to ripen the wood. A compost of 2 parts of fibrous loam to 1 part of well-decayed manure and leafmould with a good handful of sand per bushel of the mixture is suitable. Prune in February. Propagation is by seed sown in spring in a temperature of up to 70°F (21 C) but it is more usual to propagate by cuttings. Take young shoots 2–3 inches long in spring and insert with bottom heat of 60 F (16 C) reducing it to 50–60 F (10–16 C) about 3 weeks later. Pot up the cuttings, pinching in between shifts, as required.

**Training fuchsias** Stopping during the spring is required, whatever, form the plants are to take, but if they are destined to be standards they must, from the beginning, be confined to a single stem and all sideshoots rubbed away, until the main stem is 3½ feet high. Then all the sideshoots that grow from this head must be stopped.

To form a bush or pyramid, every sideshoot should be stopped at the third joint until enough branches are produced.

Fan training combines the two ideas, laterals are trained in to a frame and sideshoots pinched out. It takes eighteen months to produce a good trained form and there is no short cut, but the finished article is something of immense charm and fascination.

### Gynura (ji-neu-ra)
From the latin *gyne*, female, *oura*, tail, the stigma being long and rough *(Compositae)*. A small genus of greenhouse perennials, native of tropical regions of India and Asia, grown for their ornamental foliage. The flower heads are solitary or in corymbs and are in varying shades of orange.

**Species cultivated** *G. aurantiaca*, 2–3 feet, stem and leaves covered with violet hairs which show especially on young plants, flowers brilliant orange in February. *G. sarmentosa,* a loosely twining plant, stems and foliage covered with dark purplish red hairs, flowers are

orange and numerous. Frequently grown as a house plant.

**Cultivation** Pot plants in March in a compost of equal parts peat, loam, of leafmould and sand, and water freely throughout the summer and moderately after October. Maintain a winter temperature of 55–65°F (13–18°C). Propagation is by cuttings taken in March and April.

### Hedera (hed-er-a)
The ancient Latin name *(Araliaceae)*. Ivy. A small genus of evergreen climbing or trailing plants which attach themselves to supports by means of aerial

roots. They are grown for their leathery, often decorative, variegated leaves. They were planted extensively in Victorian gardens, and there has been a renewed interest in them in recent years. Several species and hybrids are now used as house plants. When plants reach the top of their support they cease to produce aerial roots, growth becomes bushy, the leaves lack lobes and the plants produce flowers and fruits (usually black). Cuttings taken from mature growth will not revert to the climbing plant habit, but will remain bushy.

**Species cultivated** *H. canariensis,* Canary Island ivy, vigorous climber. 3-5 lobed leaves up to 8 inches across, leathery; vars. *azorica,* leaves with 5-7 lobes, tender; *variegata,* leaves green and silvery-grey, margined with white. *H. chrysocarpa,* Italian ivy, leaves 4 inches wide, fruits yellow. *H. colchica,* Persian ivy, strong growing, leaves up to 8 inches long, 4 inches wide, dark green; var. *dentata,* leaves toothed, *dentata variegata,* variegated yellow. *H. helix,* common ivy, a native plant which may grow 80-100 feet up trees, leaves variable in size and number of lobes; vars. *aureo-variegata,* leaves flushed yellow; 'Buttercup' (also known as 'Golden Cloud' and 'Russell's Gold'), small leaves, flushed yellow; *caenwoodiana,* small, narrowly lobed leaves; 'Chicago', large leaves, 3-lobes; 'Chicago' *variegata,* variegated cream; *conglomerata,* slow growing, growth dense,

**1** The leaves of Gynura sarmentosa are covered with purple-red hairs.
**2** Hedera helix 'Chicago', a cream variegated form grown as a pot plant.
**3** Helxine soleirolii, 'Baby's Tears', is grown for its attractive leaves.
**4** Hippeastrum evansii, a charming yellow and white species of this South American plant which is closely related to Amaryllis.

leaves small, wavy, suitable for rock garden; *congesta,* slow growing, growth dense, leaves more or less triangular, grey-green; *deltoidea,* leaves 3-lobed, the two basal ones overlapping; *digitata,* leaves broad, 5-lobed; *discolor,* small leaves, flushed red, mottled with cream; 'Eva', leaves small, margined cream, variegation very variable; 'Glacier', leaves grey, margined cream; *gracilis,* graceful, slender growth; 'Jubilee' (or 'Golden Leaf'), small leaves, central vein red, yellow mark at base; 'Little Diamond', central lobe long pointed, variegated cream and pale green; *lutzii,* dense growth, lime green and cream, darker green flecks; *palmata,* slow growing, palmately lobed leaves; 'Pittsburgh' mid-green, cream veins; *purpurea,* leaves bronze-purple in winter; 'Shamrock', very dark green leaves, basal lobes overlapping; *tortuosa,* curled and twisted leaves; *tricolor,* leaves grey-green, edged white, rosy in winter. Other varieties and cultivars may be offered in trade lists from time to time.

*H. hibernica,* Irish ivy, strong growing, large leaves up to 6 inches wide, bright green in colour, usually 5-lobed, useful for ground cover under trees and in other shady places.

**Cultivation** Ivies will grow in any aspect out doors and in any kind of soil. Plant in autumn or early spring. When used as ground cover peg the shoots to the soil to encourage growth. Prune in April and feed as required for rapid growth. When grown in pots indoors John Innes potting compost No. 1 is suitable; provide good drainage. Plants may be allowed to trail, may be trained up sticks or bark-covered branches or trained to a fan or frame of any form. Water moderately in winter; freely in summer, when established plants should be fed occasionally. It should be noted that the varieties are more often grown as house plants and as such are liable to damage by frost.

**Helxine** (helks-in-e)
Derivation uncertain. Possibly from the ancient Greek name for pellitory, a related plant, or from the Latin *helix,* ivy, since the plant creeps (*Urticaceae*). Baby's tears. A genus of a single species from Corsica, *H. soleirolii,* a nearly hardy, creeping perennial with insignificant flowers, grown for its attractive tiny, bright green leaves. It is quick growing and useful for dry walls and among paving stones in mild districts; it can become invasive but is easily blackened by frost; however, usually not all the plant is killed. It is particularly useful in cold greenhouses as an edging to staging or in pots or hanging baskets for conservatories. The plant grows about 2–3 inches tall. The varieties 'Silver Queen', with silver variegated foliage, and 'Golden Queen' with yellow variegation, are also attractive.

**Cultivation** Ordinary garden soil to which a little leafmould has been added at planting time is suitable. Dry banks, rock work, dry walls in sun or shade are all suitable positions. It makes a good pot plant for patios, conservatories or cold greenhouses in a compost of 1 part of loam and 1 part of leafmould. Pot in spring and water moderately. Propagation is easy by division in spring.

**Hippeastrum** (hip-pe-as-trum)
Derived from the Greek *hippeus,* a knight, *astron,* a star, possibly in connection with a resemblance to knights and stars as seen in *H. equestre* (*Amaryllidaceae*). A genus of S. American, greenhouse, bulbous plants often referred to as *Amaryllis,* to which they are closely related. The large, showy, trumpet flowers of the hybrids, ranging in colour from the richest velvety crimson to the more delicate shades of pink and white, also bicolored, rank them among the most prized of winter and spring flowering pot plants for the greenhouse. Most of the hippeastrums

## 3 Hoya (hoy-a)

Commemorating Thomas Hoy, gardener to the Duke of Northumberland at Syon House, Chiswick in the late eighteenth century (*Asclepiadaceae*). A genus of evergreen climbing or trailing shrubs for a cool greenhouse or stove house. All have clusters of wax-like flowers.

**Species cultivated** *H. bella,* 3 feet, white and crimson flowers, summer, stove-house. *H: carnosa,* honey plant, wax flower, climber to 10–12 feet, fragrant pink and white flowers, summer; var. *variegata,* leaves variegated.

**Cultivation** Plants can be set out direct into the greenhouse border in good loamy soil with plenty of peat and sand and a little crushed charcoal added, or can be put into large pots or tubs and repotted in the spring. The twining shoots are trained up pillars or trellisses or against walls. *H. carnosa* does not need high temperatures and may be used as a house plant or grown in a slightly heated conservatory. Over-crowded shoots should be thinned out. Hoyas like sunny positions. It is important not to remove the flower stalks after the flowers have faded as a second crop of flowers will be produced upon them. Cuttings from shoots of the previous year's growth can be taken from March to late May and rooted in a propagating case with bottom heat, or shoots can be layered in autumn.

## Hypocyrta (hi-po-sir-ta)

From the Greek *hypo,* under, and *kyrtos,* curved, alluding to the flower being swollen on the under side (*Gesneriaceae*). A genus of about 12 species of shrubs, mostly from Brazil, which require warm greenhouse treatment in the British Isles.

**Species cultivated** *H. glabra,* 1–2 feet, an erect shrub, scarlet and yellow flowers, June and July, South America. *H. pulchra,* 6 inches, flowers scarlet and yellow, June, most decorative leaves, dull green above with brown markings, wine-red beneath, Colombia.

**Cultivation** These plants should be given warm greenhouse treatment and shaded from bright sun. Pot moderately firmly in a compost consisting of peat and leaf-soil with a little loam and sand. The winter temperature should not drop below 55°F (13°C). Propagate by cuttings of young shoots inserted in moist peat, or by mature leaf cuttings, in a propagating case with bottom heat.

## Impatiens (im-pa-she-ens, or im-pat-e-ens)

From the Latin *impatiens* in reference to the way in which the seed pods of some species burst and scatter their seed when touched (*Balsaminaceae*). Balsam, or Busy Lizzie. A genus of about 500 species of annuals, biennials and sub-shrubs mostly from the mountains of Asia and Africa. The succulent hollow

---

offered in trade lists are of hybrid origin.

**Species cultivated** *H. aulicum,* 2 feet, crimson and purple flowers, winter. *H. pardinum,* 2 feet, flowers green, yellow and scarlet, spring. *H. pratense,* 2 feet, scarlet flowers, spring and early summer. *H. procerum,* 3 feet, bluish-mauve flowers, spring. *H. psittacinum,* 2 feet, flowers orange and scarlet, summer. *H. puniceum* (syn. *H. equestre*), Barbados lily, 18 inches, red flowers, summer. *H. reginae,* 2 feet, red and white flowers, spring. *H. reticulatum,* 1 foot, flowers rose or scarlet, spring. *H. rutilum,* 1 foot, crimson and green flowers, spring. *H. vittatum,* 2 feet, flowers crimson and white, spring. Cultivars include 'Fire Dance', vermilion; 'Picotee', pure white, petals edged red; 'Queen of the Whites', faintly grey inside; 'Rilona', pure salmon; 'Wyndham Hayward', dark red, deeper inside.

**Cultivation** Pot new bulbs in January, choosing a pot size to leave no more than ¾ inch width of soil between the bulb and the pot rim. Bulbs should be planted to half their depth only, in John Innes No 2 compost, or a mixture of 2 parts of turfy loam, and 1 part of sharp sand, plus a double handful of bonemeal to each bushel of the mixture. Start them into growth in a temperature of 60°F (16°C) and give no water for the first two weeks, then start with small amounts. As flower spikes appear, within about 3 weeks of being started, the temperature

---

**1 Hippeastrum 'Wyndham Hayward,' a beautiful dark red variety.**
**2 and 3 Two typical species of the brittle stemmed Impatiens. Impatiens roylei, on the left, has attractive buds and well-marked flowers in June.**

can rise to 65–70°F (18–21°C) by day, with a night minimum of 60°F (16°C). Keep the plants well watered and fed with liquid manure while growing, syringeing twice daily and maintaining a humid atmosphere. Remove dead flower heads if seed is not required. Gradually reduce the water supply from July to September (according to the time the bulbs were started into growth) until the pots are stored dry in a minimum temperature of 40°F (4°C) for winter. Examine and repot as necessary in January, removing all dead roots. Renew the surface compost of bulbs not repotted, and start them into growth.

Young plants raised from seed should not be dried off for the winter until after their first flowering, but will need less water while the older bulbs are resting. Sow seed as soon as it is ripe, in a temperature of 60–65°F (16–18°C). Grow on in quantities in large pots or boxes until plants are about 6 inches tall, then pot them individually into 4-inch pots for their first flowering. Named or selected forms are increased by offsets removed and potted separately when the plants are inspected in January.

stems are brittle and much branched. Few species are now cultivated, those that are may be grown in flower borders or under glass, or in the home as house plants.

**Species cultivated** *I. balsamina,* 1½ feet, rose, scarlet and white, summer, annual, greenhouse. *I. holstii,* 2–3 feet, scarlet, almost continuous flowering, half-hardy, greenhouse perennial; var. Imp Series F₁, low growing, brilliant mixed colours, in shade and sun. *I. petersiana,* 1 foot, reddish-bronze leaves and stems, red, almost continuous flowering, half-hardy, greenhouse perennial. *I. sultanii,* 1–2 feet, rose and carmine, almost continuous flowering, greenhouse perennial. *I. amphorata,* 5 feet, purple, August, annual. *I. roylei* (syn. *I. glandulifera),* 5 feet, purple or rose-crimson, spotted flowers in profusion, summer, annual.

**Cultivation** Greenhouse plants are potted in a mixture of equal parts loam, leaf-mould and sharp sand in well-drained pots, during February or March. They do best in well-lit conditions, and require moderate watering March–September, but only occasionally otherwise. They

**1 Hoya carnosa in its most favoured position – clambering up supports to the top of a greenhouse where it enjoys any sunshine available.
2 Mammillaria bocasana grows in groups and has silky white hairs and hooks from the areoles all over the plant. The flowers are papery and shades of silver-pink in colour.
3 A group of Mammillaria geminispina.**

require a temperature of 55–65°F (13–18°C) from October to March, 65–75°F (18–24°C) March to June, and about 65°F (18°C) for the rest of the time. Pinch back the tips to make them bushy during February. Hardy species do well in ordinary soil in a sunny position, about 6 inches apart. *I. holstii* can be grown as a bedding plant and prefers light shade out of doors; it will tolerate varied temperatures. Propagate by seed in spring, sown in heat for the greenhouse species, and out of doors where the plants are to grow, for the hardy species, or by cuttings taken March to August, and placed in sandy soil in a temperature of 75°F (24°C).

## Mammillaria (mam-mil-lar-e-a)

From the Latin *mamma,* the breast, or *mamilla,* nipple, in reference to the teat-like tubercles of many species *(Cactaceae).* A large genus of greenhouse succulent perennials, suitable for window culture. Most species are from the southern parts of North America and Mexico and can be recognised by the numerous tubercles covering them; there are no ribs as on many globular cacti. They are mostly dwarf plants forming large groups *(caespitose),* but there are a few taller ones. Mammillarias have areoles between the tubercles from which flowers arise; they also have areoles on the tops of the tubercles from which the species arise. Offsets can form from either type of areole. The flowers are produced in rings near the growing centre between the tubercles (axils). No more flowers will appear at the areole where it has already borne a flower and so fresh growth must be encouraged each year.

**Species cultivated** There are over 300 species and many varieties—the following is a mere selection: *M. albicans,* densely covered with white spines, red flowers. *M. bocasana,* grouping, with silky white hairs and red hooks, flowers pink. *M. camptotricha,* pale green body with golden twisting spines, white flowers. *M. decipiens,* grouping, large tubercles with red spines, flowers pink or white. *M. elongata,* finger-like stems, many varieties, flowers white. *M. fraileana,* tall-growing with strong hooks, large pink flowers. *M. gracilis,* small type with offsets which fall readily, flowers yellowish. *M. hahniana,* very attractive, with long white hairs, red flowers, *M. innae,* small-growing, white-spined species, red flowers. *M. jaliscana,* globular, freely offsetting with large pinkish-red flowers. *M. karwinskiana,* open type with strong spines, cream coloured inner petals. *M. longiflora,* very long thin tubercles, many thin spines, long tubed pink flowers, central spine hooked. *M. magnimamma,* open type with many varieties, strong spines, flowers cream. *M. nunezii,* columnar growing, many fine spines, red flowers. *M. orcuttii,* dense white wool at top with dark spines, flowers pale red with darker mid-rib. *M. plumosa,* handsome species with feather-like spines, flowers pink, December. *M. quevedoi,* globular with white spines and wool at top. *M. rhodantha,* columnar growth with brassy spines, flowers pink. *M. spinosissima,* tall cylindrical type with many spines, yellow, brown, or red, flowers purplish. *M. tetracantha,* open type, with stiff spines, flowers pink. *M. uncinata,* open type with a hooked spine at each areole, flowers pink. *M. vaupelii,* covered with yellow and brown short spines, attractive. *M. wildii,* common species with yellow spines and hooks, flowers white. *M. xanthina,* rare species with strong hooks. *M. yaquensis,* small type making groups with fierce hooks. *M. zeilmanniana,* the most free-flowering species, with soft tubercles and cerise flowers.

**Cultivation** Grow mammillarias in John Innes potting compost No 2 with ⅙ part of sharp sand, grit and broken brick added. Repot in March or April, once every year or two; do not use a large pot. Water well from March to October, as often as the soil dries out, but do not give any water from October to February. The temperature in winter should be 40°F (4°C) and in summer 65–85°F (18–30°C). Some species, from Baja, California and the West Indies, require a higher winter temperature. Some open types need a little shade from strong sunshine. Plants are easily raised from seed sown in pans of John Innes seed compost in February in a temperature of 70°F (21°C). Keep the pans of seedlings at this temperature, moist and shaded. Offsets may also be rooted in a mixture of sharp sand and peat in equal parts. Some species may be increased by detaching and rooting tubercles.

## Maranta (mar-ant-a)

Commemorating B. Maranti, an Italian botanist *(Marantaceae)*. This genus contains 30 species, all natives of tropical America. One important economic product, the West Indian arrowroot, is prepared from the rhizomes of *M. arundinacea.* However, those species which are cultivated under glass in Britain are valued for the sake of their decorative leaves.

**Species cultivated** *M. arundinacea variegata,* 6 feet, leaves green and white. *M. bicolor,* 1 foot, leaves olive green, Brazil. *M. chantrieri,* 1 foot, leaves grey and dark green. *M. leuconeura,* 1 foot, leaves green, white and purple; vars. *kerchoveana,* green and dark red leaves; *massangeana,* green and rosy-purple.

**Cultivation** All need stove treatment and

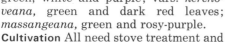

1 Maranta leuconeura kerchoveana has green leaves with deep rosy purple markings. The plant sometimes has small white flowers. They can be grown as houseplants as long as the temperature does not fall below 10°C and the atmosphere remains moist.
2 The flower of Monstera deliciosa has honeycomb markings within the spathe and originally comes from Mexico.
3 One of the many forms of Nephrolepis exaltata, commonly known as the Boston Fern.
4 A crested form of Nephrolepis exaltata.
5 Nephrolepis exaltata and its various forms are best grown in baskets hung from the roof of a greenhouse. The soil mixture must be kept moist and the winter temperature should not drop below about 13°C.

some shade from full sun, if they are grown under glass. They are also grown as houseplants and will succeed provided the room temperature does not fall below 50°F (10°C) and a moist atmosphere is provided round the leaves by standing the pots in other containers filled with water-absorbent material such as peat, which is kept moist. They do best in shady rooms or in shady corners of well-lit rooms. Water in abundance is required from March to October, and plants should be syringed daily during this period. Keep the soil on the dry side from October to March. A suitable compost consists of 1 part of loam, 2 parts of peat, 1 part of sand, in well-drained pots. The temperature from February to October should be 60–70°F (16–21°C), October to February 55–65°F (13–18°C). Repot the plants in spring after their winter rest. Propagation is by careful division of the rhizomes or tubers at potting time.

## Monstera (mon-ster-a)

Possibly so named because the perforated leaves of some species are rather unusual and may perhaps be considered monstrosities (Araceae). A genus of about 30 species of evergreen climbers from tropical America and the West Indies. A few species only are cultivated and one, at least, M. deliciosa, makes an excellent house plant where the temperature of the room is suitable. The leaves are very large and in some species there are curious indentations and perforations. Aerial roots are produced along the stems and these attach themselves to supports. They need a warm greenhouse but when established can be transferred to a living room. The fruit of M. deliciosa is sometimes obtainable and has a pineapple flavour. Species cultivated M. acuminata, flattened stem, leaves to 10 inches long, Guatemala. M. deliciosa, deep green leaves, to 2 feet across, perforated, flowers yellowish, Mexico. M. pertusa, very variable species, leaves to 16 inches long, perforated, tropical America.

Cultivation When grown in a warm greenhouse these plants do best in a border and must be provided with some support upon which to climb. They like a compost of peat, leafmould, loam and some sand, or they can be grown in John Innes No 1 potting compost. Syringe daily and water freely in the summer months. A temperature of 55–65°F (13–18°C) should be maintained in the winter months. They are best planted in the spring and can be propagated by stem cuttings taken at any time during the year and rooted in a temperature of 70–80°F (21–27°C) using a sandy compost.

## Nephrolepis (neff-ro-lep-iss)

From the Greek *nephros*, a kidney, *lepis*, a scale, referring to the shape of the covering of the spore-cases *(Polypodiaceae)*. Ladder fern. A genus of about 30 species of ferns, widely distributed over tropical regions, grown for their beautiful fronds. There are both terrestrial and epiphytic kinds. Young plants are produced on the stolons and as with age the crowns become weak and the fronds become much shorter, these young plants can be detached and potted on.

**Species cultivated** *N. acutifolia*, fronds to 2 feet long, 4 inches broad, Malaya. *N. cordifolia*, fronds to 2 feet long, 2 inches broad, tropics, Japan, New Zealand. *N. duffii*, fronds to 2 feet long, Australia, Malaya. *N. exaltata*, fronds to 2 feet long or more, 6 inches broad, tropics; there are many cultivars known as Boston ferns, some with much-divided fronds, others crested. They include 'Anna Foster', *elegantissima, hillii, wredei*. These cultivars sometimes revert to the species, so that when young plants are selected for purposes of propagation, it is necessary to ensure that the right stock is chosen. *N. hirsutula*, similar to *N. exaltata*, but with reddish-brown rachises (stalks of the fronds), tropics.

**Cultivation** The best way to grow these plants is in baskets suspended from the roof of the house in a compost of 3 parts of peat, 1 part of loam and 1 of sand and given a liquid nitrogenous feed once a week during the growing season.

Scale insects are the only pests which attack these ferns. These can be controlled by using malathion at the rate of ½ oz to 2 gallons of water. Make sure, too, that all material is clean when propagating.

These plants do very well in a temperature of 55–60°F (13–16°C) during the winter months, slightly higher during summer. They must not be allowed to dry out at any time. Except for *N. duffii*, which is sterile, the species may be raised from spores as described in the article Fern cultivation. *N. duffii* may be propagated by division, as may the other species and cultivars.

## Nertera (ner-ter-a)

From the Greek *nerteros*, referring to the prostrate habit of the plant *(Rubiaceae)*. Bead plant. There are about 6 species in the genus, herbaceous perennials of creeping habit, natives of mountains in many parts of the southern hemisphere. There is one species only in common cultivation, *N. granadensis* (syn. *N. depressa*). It is a low-growing, spreading plant, its main decorative feature being its dense crop of bright orange, pea-sized berries. Coming from New Zealand, Australia and South America, it is almost hardy in Britain and is sometimes grown permanently on rock gardens, with winter protection.

1

2

Cultivation *N. granadensis* is normally grown as a greenhouse pot plant, in sandy compost, such as 2 parts of sandy loam, 1 part each of sand and leafmould. Plants should be shaded from strong sunlight. Pot in spring in warmth and afterwards, when the plants are established, move the pots to a cool place to assist flower and berry formation. Keep the plants well watered. Out of doors they may be grown on shady parts of the rock garden in ordinary light rich soil, but will need some protection in winter. They are easily raised from seed sown in warmth in spring or may be increased by potting small pieces separated from established plants.

## Notocactus (no-to-kak-tus)

From the Greek *notos*, south, and *cactus*, but for obscure reasons *(Cactaceae)*. A genus of 15 species of greenhouse succulent perennials, from sub-tropical South America. Most species are very free-flowering and popular with collectors. Many can be flowered easily on a sunny windowsill.

**Species cultivated** *N. apricus*, stem globular, depressed, shallow ribs with curved spines, not sharp, flowers large, yellow with reddish outer petals, Uruguay. *N. concinnus*, similar in shape to previous species, very free-flowering, yellow flowers with red stigma, southern

Brazil. *N. floricomus*, stem globular when young becoming columnar, flowers freely produced, satin-like, yellow, Uruguay. *N. graessneri*, a very handsome species with pale green stem and many golden spines, likes semi-shade, flowers greenish-yellow, southern Brazil. *N. haselbergii*, another fine species, dense white spines on body, flowers tomato-red, can last three weeks, southern Brazil. *N. leninghausii*, one of the tallest species, golden spines, flowers yellow, southern Brazil. *N. rutilans*, dark green body, white radial spines, darker centrally, flowers pale mauve to rosy red. *N. schumannianus*, tall-growing species, woolly at top, rather long spines, flowers yellow, northern Argentina. *N. scopa*, stem cylindrical, many radial spines, flowers bright yellow, southern Brazil.

**Cultivation** A suitable soil mixture consists of John Innes Potting No 2, with $\frac{1}{6}$ part added of sharp sand, grit and broken brick. Pot in March every year or two, and give the plants a sunny place in the greenhouse or window. Water as often as the soil dries out, from March to September, but keep the soil dry in winter. Maintain a minimum winter temperature of 40 F (4 C) rising in summer to 65–75 F (18–24 C). Propagation is by seed sown in pans of John Innes seed compost in February. Keep

**1 The New Zealand plant Nertera granadensis is a low-growing species which produces these orange berries.**
**2 Notocactus tabulare has unusually attractive flowers.**
**3 Notocactus apricus has a globular spiny stem with reddish outer petals.**
**4 Brazil's Notocactus leninghausii grows taller than any of the other species.**
**5 Another of this attractive species – Notocactus rutilans.**

73

the seed pans shaded and moist, at a temperature of 70 F (21 C), prick out the seedlings when the cotyledon has been absorbed. Offsets which form at the base of some plants can be removed and rooted in a mixture of sharp sand and peat.

## Opuntia (o-pun-tee-a)

From the Greek *Opuntus*, a town in Greece where cactus-like plants are said to have grown *(Cactaceae)*. Prickly pear. A genus of greenhouse succulent plants which can also be grown in a sunny window. This is a very large genus of between 250 and 300 species, natives of the Americas and the Galapagos Islands. The plants vary in shape from having small cylindrical joints to large flat pads or tree-like growths. Some retain a small cylindrical leaf at the areole for some time. The flowers are mostly spreading and colourful, the fruits are quite often edible. For a cactus, they have large seeds. The areoles carry glochids—small tufts of short spines—and as they are barbed they are easily picked up on the fingers.

**Greenhouse species cultivated** *O. brasiliensis*, tree-like stem with pale green flat joints, flowers pale yellow, widely distributed in Brazil and Bolivia. *O. cylindrica*, stems tall and round with few white spines, flowers red, Ecuador, Peru. *O. dillenii*, makes a large bush, yellow glochids, large yellow flowers, West Indies, Mexico. *O. elongata*, tree-like in growth, stems oval-long, few spines, flowers wide, pale yellow, Mexico. *O. ficus-indica*, 15 feet, canary yellow flowers, bears fruits which are edible and much appreciated in America, but they

have fine glochids on them which must be removed before eating, large oval pads are formed with few spines, tropical America. *O. herrfeldtii*, an erect bushy plant with a short stem, handsome species, reddish-brown glochids, flowers sulphur yellow, Mexico. *O. grandiflora*, few spines, large flowers 4 inches across, yellow with a red centre, eastern Texas. *O. macracantha*, cylindrical stem with long spines, flowers orange-yellow, Cuba. *O. microdasys*, a much branched bush, very popular for window cultivation or bowl gardens, almost round pads well covered with glochids, no long spines, flowers pale yellow with reddish tips to petals, northern Mexico; there are several varieties of this species varying according to the colour of the glochids, a white one known as *alba*, red known as *rufida*, and a pale yellow known as *pallida*. All sensitive to low winter temperatures. *O. sulphurea*, joints oval or elliptical, glochids yellowish-red, a very popular species, Argentina.

**Hardy** *O. engelmannii*, spreading bush, joints oval or round, flower yellow, 4 inches across, central America. *O. polyacantha*, one of the hardiest opuntias, the pads are broadly oval and sprawl over the ground, it has many areoles close together, and whitish spines, flowers pale yellow; there are several varieties with differing coloured spines, British Columbia and Arizona. *O. vulgaris* (syn. *O. opuntia*), thick joints growing prostrate, flowers pale yellow, North America.

**Greenhouse species cultivation** A compost mixture consisting of John Innes potting compost No 2 with $\frac{1}{6}$ part added of sharp sand, grit and broken brick is suitable.

Pot them in spring in a well-drained pot, just large enough to take the roots and give them a sunny position in the greenhouse or a sunny windowsill. Water them from March to September, fairly freely when new growth is seen, but do not give so much that the soil remains very wet for long periods. From October to March they should not be watered at all, unless they are being grown in a heated room, when they can be watered once a month. A temperature of not less

than 45°F (7°C) is required in winter, rising to 65–80°F (18–27°C) in summer.

**Hardy species cultivation** These must have a well-drained soil as the plants will not stand a permanently wet position. Although some opuntias will stand the winter out of doors in England it must be realised that a severe winter could kill them. A sheltered spot must be found and some shelter from too much rain will help them to survive. Propagate all kinds by seed sown in John Innes seed compost. Cover the seeds as they are usually large, and then keep them damp, shaded and at a temperature of 70°F (21°C). Do not discard the seed pan if no seedlings appear for some time, as the seeds can still germinate after a year. Propagation may also be effected by cuttings which can be taken off at pads or joints, the base dried in the sun and set in sharp sand. Spray them occasionally and keep them in a sunny position.

## Pelargonium (pel-ar-go-knee-um)

From the Greek *pelargos,* a stork, referring to the resemblance between the beak of the fruit and that of a stork *(Geraniaceae).* This is the correct name for the plant which is grown in public parks and our gardens and greenhouses. The zonal pelargoniums have in the past 70 years mostly been called 'Geraniums' which is a complete misnomer.

Within the past 10 years the horticultural public has been made aware of the misnomer, mainly by the efforts of the specialist societies throughout the world, and are now using the correct term for the zonal and regal pelargoniums in increasing numbers.

To help to sort out the confusion that has existed it is worth stating that the cultivars of the genus *Pelargonium,* both regal and zonal types, have definitely been bred from the true *Pelargonium* species and not from the genus *Geranium;* this is the key to the correct definition.

In the genus *Pelargonium* there are over 300 recorded species; this does not include the sub-species and other varieties not recorded yet, of which there must be a considerable number.

1 **Opuntia speggazzinii with its silvery-white flowers.**
2 **The Prickly Pear, or basic Opuntia.**
3 **Opuntia bergeriana has deep red flowers and is the plant that commonly forms thickets on the Riviera.**
4 **Opuntia paraguensis with its deep, golden, cup-shaped flowers.**
5 **The Mediterranean Opuntia bergeriana.**
6 **Opuntia microdasys.**

The species are identified in one way by the fact that the plants breed true from seed, although some have individual races within the species which also breed true from seed and a lot of cross-pollination is done by insects on plants growing in their natural habitat, causing much confusion among taxonomists. Many of these natural hybrids are very closely identified with the original plant but may have slightly different leaves, form or flowers.

The species were mainly brought to England from many parts of Africa, although several places in other parts of the world have also contributed, such as Australia, New Zealand and Tasmania, during the last three centuries. They are not hardy here and have to be protected during the winter months, although a wide range of species is grown out of doors in the Abbey Gardens at Tresco, Isles of Scilly.

What is so remarkable is that such a large number of colourful cultivated varieties could ever have been bred from plants that have only very small flowers. It shows the tenacity and enthusiasm of the breeders who performed this task, mainly during the last century, although this work has been carried on into the present era.

The species are fascinating to explore and there is no doubt that they are more important than the cultivars in many ways, especially in their use for hybridising purposes and also for experimentation and research.

There are all kinds of fantastic shapes and forms among the various kinds and a great number have perfume in their leaves. Although this scent is often clearly defined it cannot be assessed absolutely in all varieties because so many factors have to be taken into consideration, which contribute to the amount of volatile oil in the tissues. Variations of this can be caused by environment, feeding, soil structure, age of plants, time or season of year, etc., all of which can vary from county to county and country to country. One of the main reasons why smells or perfumes seem to vary is because the sense of smell varies widely between one person and another.

The volatile oil is distilled from many of the species to be used in cosmetics and perfumes.

The leaves of the pelargonium are edible and are used a great deal in cooking and can add at least ten different flavours to any cake or sweetmeat. It is, therefore, worthwhile growing certain species for this purpose alone.

**Cultivation** In general pelargoniums grown in pots will do well in the John Innes potting composts, though it is advisable to add a little extra lime to neutralise the acidity of the peat. Alternatively, particularly for potting on rooted cuttings, a suitable soil mixture consists of 2 parts of good loam, 1 part of sand, 1 part of peat, all parts by bulk, not weight, plus 1 pint of charcoal and 1 cupful of ground limestone per bushel of the mixture. The ingredients should be thoroughly mixed together and then watered with a liquid fertiliser with a high potash content. Some growers have been successful with the 'no-soil' composts (peat/sand mixtures plus balanced fertilisers), while others use ordinary good garden soil which has been cleared of worms and sterilised to kill harmful soil organisms.

Pelargoniums should never be over-potted. When repotting becomes necessary it is often possible, by removing old compost and slightly reducing the size of the root-ball, to repot into pots of the same size; otherwise the plants should be moved into pots one size larger only. They should always be potted firmly.

Although plants should be watered freely during the growing period, in spring and summer, they should never be over-watered and, in any case, the pots in which they are grown should be properly crocked and the soil mixture should be free-draining so that surplus moisture can get away quickly, otherwise various root-rots and stem-rots may be encouraged. In winter plants will need little water, though the soil in the pots should not be allowed to dry out.

Some shading will be required in the greenhouse from late April or early May onwards. A light application of 'Summer Cloud' or other proprietary shading compound to the glass will be sufficient.

In order to prevent damping-off of the flowers the atmosphere in the greenhouse should be kept as dry as possible during the summer. This means that proper use should be made of the ventilators and that every attempt should be made to keep the air circulating to avoid an over-humid, stagnant atmosphere. During the winter, when it is equally important to keep the air dry, though warm, good circulation can be provided by using an electrical blower heater.

To keep the plants growing freely and to maintain good leaf colour it is necessary to feed them during the growing season. Regular weak applications of proprietary liquid fertiliser should be given from about a month after the plants are in their final pots, until September. It should be noted, however, that plants in the fancy-leaved group should either not be fed at all, or the feed they are given should not contain nitrogen. These kinds should, in any case, be given less water than others.

A number of zonal varieties can be induced to flower in winter, when blooms are always welcome. The method is to take cuttings in the spring, by normal propagation methods described below. The young plants are grown on steadily during the summer and all flower buds are removed until late September. Plants treated in this way should flower throughout the winter months. It is best to maintain a minimum temperature of 60°F (16°C) and the plants should be given as much light as possible. During the summer the plants may be placed in a sunny cold frame or the pots may be plunged in a sunny, sheltered place out of doors. They should be brought into the greenhouse in September.

Plants which are to be used for summer bedding purposes are raised from cuttings taken in August or September, rooting several in each 5-inch pot, or in boxes, spacing the cuttings 2 inches apart. In February the rooted cuttings are potted into individual 3-inch pots and kept in a temperature of 45–50°F (7–10°C) until April. They are then hardened off in a cold frame before planting them out of doors in late May or early June, when all danger of frost is over. Do not plant shallowly; it is best to take out a hole large enough and deep enough to take the plant up to its first pair of leaves. Leggy plants may be planted more deeply. Remove dead leaves and flowers as soon as they are seen and pinch out long, unwanted shoots from time to time to keep the plants bushy. Keep the plants well watered in dry weather. A gentle overhead spray in the evenings in hot weather is beneficial. In September, before the first frosts, the plants should be lifted and brought into the greenhouse for the winter. The shoots should be cut back, long roots trimmed and the plants potted into small pots. The minimum winter temperature in the greenhouse should be around 42°F (5°C).

Propagation of regal pelargoniums is by cuttings, which, like those of the other types, root easily. They should be about 3 inches long, taken from the top of the lateral shoots. They are trimmed back to a node and the bottom leaves are removed. They will root quickly in a sterile rooting compost, in pots or in a propagating frame in the greenhouse. Bottom heat is not required. Cuttings of this type are usually taken in July or August.

Propagation of the hortorums or zonal pelargoniums may be effected in several ways. Cuttings of the type described above may be taken and either rooted singly in 2½-inch pots or three cuttings may be inserted round the edge of a 3-inch pot. If large numbers are to be rooted they may be inserted in a suitable rooting compost in a frame, or 2 inches apart in shallow boxes. Cuttings are usually taken in June, July or August in this country, to enable them to form roots early. If they are taken later they may not root properly before the end of the season and thus may be lost. However, they may be rooted later in a propagating case in the greenhouse, and commercially they are rooted in quantity by mist propagation methods, using bottom heat.

The leaf-axil (or leaf-bud) method of taking cuttings has become popular in recent years. This consists in taking a leaf and ½ inch of stem from the parent plant, ¼ inch above and below the node or joint. The stem section is cut vertically through the centre of the stem. The cuttings thus formed are inserted in rooting compost in the normal way, just covering the buds. If some bud growth is seen in the leaf axils you are more certain of rooting the cuttings. Such cuttings are normally taken in the summer months.

Whichever method you adopt, make sure that you use clean stock only. Almost any piece of a zonal pelargonium containing stem and leaves can be used for propagation purposes, provided the conditions are right. It is quite normal to root stem cuttings of these plants out of doors during the summer months, in the open ground.

Plants may also be raised from seed obtained from a reliable source. It is unwise to buy unnamed seedlings as they may produce large plants with few flowers. Seeds should be sown $\frac{1}{16}$ inch deep in light sandy soil, in pans or boxes, in the greenhouse, from February to April, in a temperature of 55–65°F (13–18°C).

Tuberous-rooted pelargonium species may be divided in spring for propagation purposes.

The principal pests of pelargoniums grown under glass are aphids and greenhouse white fly. These may be controlled by insecticidal sprays or by fumigation methods. The disease variously known as black leg, black rot, black stem rot or pelargonium stem rot, is very liable to attack cuttings and sometimes mature plants. It first appears on the lower part of the stem, which turns black. It spreads rapidly up the stem and soon kills the plant. It seems to be encouraged by too much moisture in the compost and in over-humid conditions. Some control may be obtained by spraying or dusting plants with captan in the autumn. It is also important not to damage the skin of the stem when taking cuttings, otherwise disease spores may enter through the skin at this point. Always use a sharp sterile knife or razor blade when taking or trimming cuttings.

**Species cultivated** *P. abrotanifolium,* flowers white or rose veined with purple, leaves fragrant of southernwood (*Artemisia abrotanum*). *P. acetosum,* leaves silvery-green, tasting of sorrel, single carmine flowers, can be used in cooking. *P. angulosum,* plant hairy, leaves 5-lobed, flowers purple, veined maroon. *P. australe,* flowers rose or whitish, spotted and striped carmine, Australia, New Zealand, Tasmania. *P. capitatum,* rose scent, pale mauve blooms. *P. crispum,* strong lemon scent, flowers pink or rose; vars. *major,* larger; *minor,* smaller; *variegatum,* lemon scent, grey-green leaves with cream edges, very elegant for floral display work. *P. cucullatum,*

**Pelargonium 'Caroline Schmidt', an attractive brightly flowered variety. The zonal pelargoniums have been called Geraniums for most of the 20th-century. In recent years, however, specialist societies have encouraged the use of the correct name for this very common plant.**

rose-scented cupped leaves, flowers red with darker veins, late summer, a parent of the regal pelargoniums and very good for outdoor pot plant growing. *P. denticulatum*, sticky leaves with strong undefined scent, flowers lilac or rosy-purple, best species with fern-like foliage. *P. echinatum*, sweetheart geranium, tuberous-rooted, stems spiny, leaves heart-shaped, lobed, flowers purple, pink or white, nearly hardy. *P. filicifolium* (syn. *P. denticulatum filicifolium*), fern-like leaves, very pungent scent, small rose flowers. *P. formosum*, salmon flowers, white-tipped, upright habit. *P. × fragrans*, nutmeg-scented geranium, small dark green leaves smelling of spice, flowers white, veined red; var. *variegata*, a miniature plant with a very pleasant scent, tiny light green leaves edged with cream, easily grown and propagated, should be in every collection. *P. frutetorum*, prostrate habit, salmon flowers. *P. gibbosum*, gouty pelargonium, so named because the joints are similar to those on elderly people so afflicted, flowers greenish-yellow, early summer. *P. graveolens*, rose-scented geranium, strong rose scent, flowers pink, upper petal with dark purple spot; much used in the distillation of perfume. *P. inquinans*, scarlet flowers, plain leaves, one parent of the zonal pelargoniums. *P. multibracteatum*, leaves heart-shaped, deeply lobed, with dark green zones, flowers white. *P. odoratissimum*, apple-scented geranium, leaves heart-shaped or kidney-shaped, fragrant of apples, flowers small, white. *P. peltatum*, ivy-leaved geranium, leaves fleshy, flowers pale rosy-mauve, a parent of the ivy-leaved cultivars. *P. quercifolium*, oak-leaved geranium, leaves roughly oak-leaf shape, grey-green, strongly scented, flowers mauve. *P. radula*, fern-like leaves, fragrant of verbena, flowers rose, upper petals blotched purplish-carmine, very attractive if grown out of doors during the summer when it grows into a small shrub. *P. saxifragioides*, very dainty plant with tiny leaves similar to some ivy-leaved kinds, flowers mauve, marked purple. *P. tetragonum*, often called the cactus-type pelargonium because of its four-sided stems; its growth should be controlled by stopping because of its vigorous habit, flowers small, white, single. *P. tomentosum*, strong peppermint scent, leaves grey-green, soft and spongy, sometimes difficult to keep during the winter period, flowers tiny, white. *P. tricolor*, foliage sage green, small tricolor flowers, lower petals white, upper petals magenta, with dark spots, a good plant for pots in the greenhouse, a prize collector's piece. *P.*

1 Pelargonium 'Carisbrooke' has soft rose-pink petals with darker markings.
2 The white flowers of Pelargonium 'Muriel Harris' are feathered with red.
3 Pelargonium 'Black Prince'.

*triste,* the sad geranium, tuberous rooted, long, much-divided leaves, flowers brownish-yellow with a pale border; sweetly scented in the evening. *P. zonale,* flowers single, mauve, pink or red, leaves lightly zoned. 'Lady Plymouth', foliage as *P. graveolens* except that the leaves are variegated green and lemon. 'Mabel Grey', strong lemon scent, upright grower that needs frequent stopping. 'Prince of Orange', orange scented, small pale mauve flowers.

The 'Uniques' are another group that have sprung up in recent years and are stated to be *P. fulgidum* hybrids. *P. fulgidum,* a sub-shrubby species with bright red flowers, is prominent in their ancestry. They are best grown in pots and hanging baskets. There are many different perfumes in the leaves of the varieties listed below:
'Crimson Unique', red and black flowers; 'Scarlet Unique', lemon scent, red flowers, parent of 'Carefree' and 'Hula'; 'Paton's Unique', verbena scent, rose flowers; 'Purple Unique', peppermint scent, purple flowers; 'Rose Unique', rose scent, rose flowers; 'White Unique', white flowers with purple veins. Cultivars: one of the most important sections

1 The zonal Pelargoniums have variously coloured leaves.
2 Pelargonium 'Rapture' is apricot.
3 Pelargonium 'Blythwood', rich pansy.
4 Pelargonium 'Aztec', strawberry-red and white.
5 Pelargonium 'Lavender Grand Slam'.

of the cultivars are the regal or domesticum Pelargoniums which have very beautiful flowers and green leaves, but recently some sports have been discovered with golden and green bicolor leaves which should make these beautiful plants much sought after if hybridisers are successful in breeding these coloured leaves into this section.

The main parents of the regals are *P. cucullatum* and *P. betulinum* which are indigenous to the coastal regions of South Africa. Hybridisation started on the species mainly here in England, in France and also in central Europe well over a century ago. These plants should be grown under glass or in the house throughout the year in the British Isles, although they may be grown out of doors in summer in exceptionally protected places. Two lovely cultivars have been produced that will grow out of doors well in all kinds of weather during the summer months. These are 'Hula' and 'Carefree', from America. These two are the result of crossing the cultivars back to the species. 'Hula' and 'Carefree' do not have flower umbels as large as the true regals but have the advantage of being able to stand up to bad conditions out of doors.

1 Pelargonium 'Doris Frith' has ruffled
white flowers with deep red marking.
2 The mauve-pink flowers of
Pelargonium 'Degata'.

Some recommended cultivars are as
follows (dominating colours only are
mentioned): 'Annie Hawkins', pink;
'Applause', pink and white; 'Aztec',
strawberry pink and white; 'Blythwood',
purple and mauve; 'Caprice', pink;
'Carisbrooke', rose pink; 'Doris Frith',
white; 'Grand Slam', red; 'Marie Rober',
lavender; 'Muriel Hawkins', pink; 'Rapture', apricot; 'Rhodamine', purple and
mauve; and the outstanding sport from
'Grand Slam', 'Lavender Grand Slam'.

The flowering season of the regals has
been greatly lengthened within the last
five years by the introduction of the new
American cultivars.

A great advantage in growing plants
in this section is that they are rarely
troubled by disease. The worst pest is the
greenhouse white fly which appears at
all times and can spread rapidly. It can,
however, easily be controlled by using
a good insecticide.

The section which dominates the
genus consists of the hortorums, usually
referred to as zonals. These are divided
into many groups which are classified as
follows (selected cultivars are listed
under each heading):

Single-flowered group (normally with
not more than five petals):
'Barbara Hope', pink; 'Block', scarlet;
'Countess of Jersey', salmon; 'Doris
Moore', cherry; 'Elizabeth Angus', rose;
'Eric Lee', magenta; 'Francis James',
bicolor flowers; 'Golden Lion', orange;
'Highland Queen', pink; 'Maxim Koval-
eski', orange; 'Mrs E. G. Hill', pink;
'Pandora', scarlet; 'Pride of the West',
cerise; 'Victorious', scarlet; 'Victory',
red.

Semi-doubles:
American Irenes of various shades and
colours are extremely useful for bedding
purposes; many named cultivars are very
similar to each other. Other cultivated
varieties include 'Dagata', pink; 'Gene-
trix', pink; 'Gustav Emich', scarlet;
'King of Denmark', pink; 'Pink Bouquet', pink; 'The Speaker', red.

Double-flowered group:
'Alpine Orange', orange; 'A. M. Maine',
magenta; 'Blue Spring', red-purple;
'Double Henry Jacoby', crimson; 'Jewel',
rose; 'Jean Oberle', pink; 'Lerchenmul-
ler', cerise; 'Monsieur Emil David',
purple; 'Maid of Perth', salmon; 'Mrs
Lawrence', pink; 'Paul Reboux', red;
'Rubin' red; 'Schwarzwalderin', rose;
'Trautleib', pink.

Cactus group (single or double flowers
with quilled petals):
'Attraction', salmon; 'Fire Dragon', red;
'Mrs Salter Bevis', pink; 'Noel', white;
'Spitfire', red with silver leaves; 'Tan-
gerine', vermilion.

Rosebud group (flower buds tight and
compact, centre petals remaining un-

1 The rose-pink flowers of Pelargonium 'Mrs Lawrence'.
2 The full head of Pelargonium 'Salmon Irene' with coral-pink flowers.
3 The double white flowers of Pelargonium 'Gonzale' make a compact head.
4 Pelargonium 'Harvester' produces a consistently rounded head.

opened, like small rosebuds):
'Apple Blossom Rosebud', pink; 'Red Rambler', red; 'Rosebud Supreme', red.
Miniature group:
'Alde', pink; 'Caligula', red; 'Cupid', pink; 'Goblin', red; 'Jenifer', carmine; 'Grace Wells', mauve; 'Mephistopheles', red; 'Mandy', cerise; 'Pauline', rose; 'Piccaninny', red; 'Taurus', red; 'Timothy Clifford', salmon; 'Wendy', salmon; 'Waveney', red.
Dwarf group:
'Blakesdorf', red; 'Emma Hossler', pink; 'Fantasia', white; 'Miranda', carmine; 'Madam Everaarts', pink; 'Pixie', salmon.
Fancy-leaved group (the colours given are those of the flowers):
*Silver leaves:* 'Flower of Spring', red; 'Mrs Mappin', red; 'Mrs Parker', pink; 'Wilhelm Langguth' (syn. 'Caroline Schmidt'), red.
*Golden leaves:* 'Golden Crest'; 'Golden Orfe'; 'Verona'.
*Butterfly leaves:* 'A Happy Thought'; 'Crystal Palace Gem'; 'Madame Butterfly'.
*Bronze bicolor leaves:* 'Bronze Corrine'; 'Bronze Queen'; 'Gaiety Girl'; 'Dollar Princess'; 'Maréchal MacMahon'; 'Mrs Quilter'.

*Multi-coloured leaves:* 'Dolly Varden'; 'Lass o' Gowrie'; 'Miss Burdett-Coutts', 'Henry Cox'; 'Mrs Pollock'; 'Sophie Dumaresque'.
Ivy-leaved group:
One of the best in this group is *P. peltatum,* the original species from which this section has been derived. Cultivars are: 'Abel Carrière', magenta; 'Beatrice Cottington', purple; 'Galilee', pink; 'La France', mauve; 'L'Elegante', leaves cream and green with purple markings; 'Madame Margot', white and green leaf; and two with green leaves and white veins, 'Crocodile' and 'White Mesh'.
In general the large-flowered cultivars described above will grow under normal garden and greenhouse conditions as will the coloured-leaved cultivars, which benefit from being left out of doors during the summer months to get full sunshine and rain.
The miniature and dwarf sections are

best grown in the greenhouse in pots, or they are very useful plants to grow out of doors in containers such as window boxes or urns. They are especially good for hanging baskets when used in conjunction with ivy-leaved kinds.
Hanging baskets are very useful for enhancing a display out of doors, especially under porches. One of the best cultivars for this purpose is 'The Prostrate Boar', a newer introduction which grows very quickly and produces an abundance of flowers throughout the summer. Make sure that you get the prostrate type and not the ordinary 'Boar' which does not grow so vigorously, nor flower so freely. 'The Boar', or *P. salmonia,* is inclined to grow vertically.
*P. frutetorum* has had in the past, and should have in the future, a great influence on the pelargonium genus because of its great vigour and its ability to influence the pigments in the leaves of the many cultivars crossed with it. Among the well-known hybrids are:
'Dark Beauty'; 'Filigree'; 'Medallion'; 'Magic Lantern'; 'Mosaic', and 'The Prostrate Boar'; large flowers have now been introduced into this group.

## Pellaea (pel-le-a)

From the Greek *pellos,* dark coloured, in reference to the black stems of this plant *(Polypodiaceae).* This is a genus of greenhouse ferns, containing over 80 species, many of which come from South America and Africa, where they grow in dry places and on stony ground. They particularly like good drainage and do well on rock banks or in small hanging baskets.

**Species cultivated** *P. atropurpurea,* fronds 4–12 inches long, North America. *P. falcata,* fronds 6–18 inches, tropical Asia, Australia, New Zealand. *P. flexuosa,* 3-foot fronds, many branches, Mexico. *P. rotundifolia,* fronds 6–12 inches, good in baskets, New Zealand. *P. viridis,* fronds 1½–2 feet, West Indies; var. *macrophylla,* much larger pinnules.

**Cultivation** Give these ferns a compost of 2 parts of peat, 1 part of loam with coarse sand added, in well-drained pots placed in a well-lit but not sunny part of the greenhouse. From October to February they should be watered moderately, but freely at other times of the year. A temperature of 60–65°F (16–18°C) is required during the summer, and in winter it should not drop below 45°F (7 °C). *P. atropurpurea* can be grown out of doors in the warmer parts of the British Isles if protected in winter; this applies also to *P. falcata* and *P. rotundifolia.* Propagation is by sowing spores, or by division in spring.

## Pellionia (pel-lee-o-ne-a)

Commemorating A. M. J. Alphonse Pellion, an officer in Freycinet's voyage round the world *(Urticaceae).* This genus of some 50 species of tropical creeping or trailing herbaceous plants is of importance in the stovehouse for the beauty of its patterned and colourful leaves, rather than its flowers. The plants are particularly suitable for growing in a hanging basket, or they may be grown under the staging, or even used as a soil covering beneath a large palm or similar plant.

**Species cultivated** *P. daveauana,* dark bronze leaves overlaid with violet and a light green mid-rib, Burma and Cochin China. *P. pulchra,* leaves patterned with blackish veins and purplish tinted stems, Cochin China.

**Cultivation** Rich soil is needed and a mixture composed of equal parts of loam, leafmould, and sand is suitable. A moist, warm atmosphere is advised. The temperature from September to April should be 55–65°F (13–18°C), and from April to September 65–75°F (18–24°C). Propagation is very easily effected by taking cuttings of the shoots and rooting these under glass in a temperature of 75–80°F (24–30°C). Plants may also be divided, preferably in March or April.

## Peperomia (pep-er-o-me-a)

From the Greek *piper,* pepper, and *omorios,* similar, flowers and foliage are similar to those of the pepper plant *(Piperaceae).* This is a genus of more than 1,000 species, mostly from the warmer parts of America, of mainly trailing plants (many are epiphytic). Some of them have tough thick leaves often with variegation or contrasted veining, and are quite suited to growing in a suspended wire basket. Some species are now used as houseplants, though it helps them to flourish if they can be returned occasionally to the greenhouse for a period. The inflorescence is in the form of an erect catkin-like process, and in some instances this adds to the decorative value of the plant.

**Species cultivated** *P. argyreia* (syn. *P. sandersii*), thick metallic white leaves with veins dark green, and dark-red leaf-stalks, Brazil. *P. brevipes,* light green leaves variegated with brown, tropical America. *P. caperata,* heart-shaped corrugated leaves, white flower spikes, sometimes branching at the tips. *P. eburnea,* leaves green, veined with emerald green, Colombia. *P. glabella,* trailing red stems, oval-shaped leaves; var. *variegata,* leaves variegated with cream. *P. hederaefolia,* heart-shaped pale grey leaves with olive-green veins. *P. maculosa,* bright green leaves, stalks spotted with purple, tropical America. *P. magnoliaefolia,* thick, cream and grey-green long-oval leaves, rather thick, reddish stems; var. *variegata,* leaves variegated yellow; 'Green Gold' is a

1 **Pellionia daveauana**, a trailer with blue flowers, is good for hanging baskets.
2 **Pellaea rotundifolia** is a greenhouse fern from New Zealand.
3 **Peperomia griseo-argentea**.
4 The cream-coloured flower spikes of **Peperomia caperata** have red stems.
5 The rather thick leaves of **Peperomia magnoliaefolia** are cream and grey.

cultivar with cream and green leaves. *P. marmorata,* bright green leaves, variegated with white, erect catkin-like flowers, southern Brazil. *P. metallica,* blackish-green leaves marked with white, veins and stems reddish, Peru. *P. obtusifolia,* large, fleshy, dark green leaves to 4 inches long, with purple margins, stems also purplish, flowers white, solitary or in pairs, on red stems,

West Indies. P. 'Princess Astrid', a cultivar of unknown origin with small green leaves with a grey stripe down the midrib. *P. scandens,* trailing stems up to 5 feet long if allowed to develop fully, leaves heart-shaped; var. *variegata,* leaves margined cream, leaf stalks pink. This is the form usually available.

**Cultivation** A suitable compost for peperomias is a mixture of 2 parts of loam, 1 part of peat, 1 part of leafmould and 1 part of coarse sand. Do not overpot; they have a small root system and do not require as large pots as might be expected. The plants should be repotted in spring. Between September and March they should be watered sparingly, and not at all in cold periods. During the growing season they can be given more water, but even then do not require as much as other plants. Keep the plants in a good light, but not sunlight, and in winter give all the light possible. Overhead spraying is beneficial. The temperature in winter should

not drop below 45°F (7°C) and 50°F (10°C) is better. In summer they require 60–75°F (16–24°C). Propagation is by cuttings, or single joints with a leaf attached placed in sandy peat and kept close in a temperature of 65–75°F (18–24°C). *P. argyreia* may be propagated by cutting up leaves into several pieces and inserting the cut edges into a sand-peat mixture in a closed propagating frame with bottom heat.

**Petunia** (pe-tu-ni-a)
From *petun,* the Brazilian name for tobacco to which petunias are nearly related *(Solanaceae).* A genus of 40 species of annual or perennial herbaceous plants from South America, two of which have been crossed to produce the many named varieties given in catalogues.

**Species cultivated** The two species concerned are *P. nyctaginiflora* and *P. integrifolia,* from the Argentine, and the resultant plants, though in fact perennial, are best treated as half-hardy annuals for the open garden. They are handsome plants, very varied in colouring, marking and form, and make extremely effective and colourful displays when used as bedding plants, in sunny situations, during late summer and autumn. Cultivars include 'Bedding Alderman', dark violet; 'Blue Bee', violet-blue; 'Blue Lace', light-blue fringed flowers with violet throat; 'Blue Danube' (F₁), lavender-blue, double; 'Blue Magic' (F₂), velvety blue; 'Canadian Wonder' (F₁), double flowers, fine colour range; 'Cascade' (F₁), large-flowered, wide range of colours; 'Cheerful', bright rose; 'Cherry Tart' (F₁), rose-pink and white; 'Confetti' (F₂), wide colour range; 'Commanche Improved' (F₁), scarlet-crimson; 'Fire Chief', fiery scarlet; 'Great Victorious' (F₁), double flowers, up to 4 inches across, wide colour range; 'Gypsy Red', brilliant salmon-scarlet; 'Lavender Queen'; 'Moonglow', yellow; 'Mound Mixed', various colours, useful for bedding; 'Pink Beauty'; 'Plum Dandy' (F₁), reddish-purple; 'Red Satin' (F₁), bright red, dwarf; 'Rose Queen'; 'Salmon

1

2

4

3

'Supreme'; 'Snowball Improved'; 'Sunburst' ($F_1$), light yellow, ruffled petals; 'Tivoli', scarlet and white bicolor; 'Valentine' ($F_1$), red, double, large flowered; 'White Magic' ($F_1$). There are also strains with fimbriated (fringed) petals in various colours. It is wise to consult current seedsmen's catalogues as very many other kinds are available and new ones appear annually.

**Cultivation** For growing out of doors, petunias should be treated rather like half-hardy annuals, sowing the very fine seed carefully in boxes in February or March in the greenhouse. Use a compost of equal parts of loam, leafmould and sand or the John Innes seed compost. Make the surface firm, with a layer of finely-sifted compost on top and do not cover the seed with any further compost once it has been sown. Keep the seed boxes in a temperature of 65–75°F (18–24°C) and do not allow the soil to dry out. Transplant the seedlings when they are large enough to handle; begin to harden them off and continue this operation until the plants are set out at the beginning of June. If seed-raised plants are required for increase, overwinter the mature plants in the greenhouse, and take cuttings in the spring, placing them in a sandy compost in a frame in a temperature of 55–65°F (13–18°C). Greenhouse cultivation is similar, but cut the plants back in February or March. Water them freely during the growing season, but moderately at other times. Feed them with a liquid fertiliser twice a week while growing, and keep them in a temperature of 55–65°F (13–18°C) during the summer. In winter do not allow the temperature to fall below 40°F (4°C), and it should preferably be higher. It may be necessary to train the growths, which can be lax and rather sappy, to stakes. For cultivation in hanging baskets or window-boxes or ornamental plant containers it is best to choose such strains as 'Cascade', or 'Pendula Balcony Blended'.

Petunias are among the gayest of summer bedding plants, and although they are really perennials they are treated as half-hardy annuals in the open garden.
1 Petunia 'Cherry Pie'.
2 Petunia 'Pink Bountiful' an F₁ hybrid, with rose-pink flowers.
3 Petunia 'Cascade', an F₁ hybrid, displays a wide range of colours.
4 A Petunia cultivar with fimbriate petals and large flowers.
5 The yellow flowers of Petunia 'Moonglow' are an uncommon colour.
6 A group of mixed Petunias.
7 Petunia 'Sugar Plum'.

## Philodendron (fil-o-den-dron)

From the Greek *phileo*, to love, and *dendron*, tree, from the plant's habit of climbing up trees *(Araceae)*. This is a large genus, containing some 275 species of tropical and sub-tropical American shrubs and climbers (often epiphytic), including some attractive plants for stove treatment; many are suitable for use as houseplants. They often have highly decorative leaves and it is for these, rather than the flowers, that they are grown.

**Stovehouse species cultivated** *P. andreanum*, climber, leaves 2–3 feet long, dark shining green with copper tints, and white veins, flowers black-purple and creamy-white, Colombia (see also *P. melanochryson*). *P. bipinnatifidum*, leaves 2 feet long, bright green, broadly triangular and deeply cut to produce almost finger-like segments, flowers reddish-brown, green and white, Brazil. *P. crassinervium*, climber, leaves 2 feet long with red margins and purplish-green stalks, very thick midrib, yellow, green and red flower, May. *P. gloriosum*, climber, large leaves, deep green with white veins and pink margins, Colombia. *P. giganteum*, climber, broadly heart-shaped leaves, white and purple flowers, West Indies.

**Houseplant species cultivated** *P. cordatum*, climber, leaves heart-shaped to 1 foot long, slow growing, Brazil. *P.*

× *corsonianum*, vigorous climber, leaves heart-shaped to 9 inches long, leaf stalks spotted dark red, hybrid. *P. elegans*, climber, dark-green palm-like leaves to 21 inches long, South America. *P. fenzlii*, vigorous climber, leaves small, 3-lobed, central lobe largest, rare in cultivation, origin unknown. *P. gloriosum*, climbing or sprawling in habit, leaves heart-shaped to 9 inches long, olive-green with pale veins, Colombia. *P. ilsemanii*, slow-growing climber, leaves arrow-shaped, to 8 inches long, creamy-pink when young, dark-green variegated white when mature, origin unknown. *P. imbe*, vigorous climber, leaves arrow-shaped, to 1 foot long, leaf stalks and stems spotted purple, Brazil. *P. lacerum*, leaves to 8 inches long, deeply cut as the plant matures, West Indies. *P. laciniatum*, climber, dark-green leaves to 9 inches long, roughly triangular in shape with 5 deeply cut lobes, Brazil. *P. leichtlinii*, slow-growing climber, leaves basically rounded but with many holes, requires a warm moist atmosphere and is more suited to stovehouse cultivation. *P. mamei*, creeping habit, leaves heart-shaped, 1 foot or more long, surface wrinkled, mottled silver, Ecuador. *P. melanochryson*, climber, dark-green velvety leaves with pale purple-pink undersurface, upper surface has a golden sheen, Colombia. This is not, in fact, a true species, but the juvenile form of *P. andreanum*. *P.*

**1** Petunia 'Pink Defiance,' a delightful member of one of the most popular plant families grown today. Originally coming from South America, the name stems from the Brazilian word for tobacco, to which petunias are related.
**2** Philodendron scandens is a vigorous climber when allowed to grow naturally. It can be nipped back to keep it bushy for use as a house plant.
**3** Philodendron Burgundy (front) and Philodendron bipinnatifidum (back) make attractive house plants.

*micans*, climber or trailer, leaves heart-shaped, 3–4 inches long, purplish or reddish variegations, Central America. *P. radiatum*, vigorous climber, leaves to 2 feet long in mature plants, irregularly triangular, much incised, Mexico, Central America. *P. sagittifolium*, climber, leaves arrow-shaped, 9 inches or so long, Mexico, Central America. *P. scandens*, vigorous climber or may be grown as a bushy specimen by pinching back growths, leaves heart-shaped, to 4 inches long, tapering to a slender point, West Indies, Panama; the most popular species; var. *variegatum*, leaves variegated with cream blotches, slow-growing. *P. selloum*, shrubby, leaves deeply lobed, 1 foot long or more, Brazil, Paraguay. *P. sodiroi*, climber, heart-shaped bright green leaves with silver spots, veins violet on undersurface, also leaf stalks, tropical America. *P. squamiferum*, climber, leaves dark-green with lighter stripes, 5-lobed, leaf stalks covered with purple bristles, Guyana, Brazil. *P. verrucosum*, climber, heart-shaped leaves dark green with darker olive-green patches, pale green on the undersurface with maroon patches, thick green bristles on stalk, Colombia, Costa Rica. *P. wendlandii*, leaves 1 foot long, oblong and shining, Costa Rica, Panama.

**Cultivation** Stove or warm greenhouse treatment is needed with a humid atmosphere, though the species listed as being suitable houseplants will grow under room conditions. *P. scandens* is the toughest for this purpose and will survive, though not grow vigorously, in rooms where the temperature falls quite low at night to around 45°F (7°C). The others need warmer, more equable conditions and a fair amount of room. All kinds grown as houseplants appreciate being removed from time to time to the moist atmosphere of a greenhouse. An open soil composed of loam and coarse peat and some sand suits these plants and a few lumps of charcoal may well be added to the soil in the pots. Give them sufficient shade to prevent scorching. Much water and some syringeing are appreciated in summer and even in winter the plants must not be allowed to get dry. Propagate by cuttings of stems in a propagating frame with a temperature of 75°F (24°C) and a very moist atmosphere.

## Pilea (py-le-a)

From the Latin *pileus,* the Roman felt cap, because of the calyx covering the achene *(Urticaceae).* A genus of about 400 species of tender perennial herbaceous plants widely distributed in the tropics. They are grown in the stovehouse and their main function is as a foil for other plants with brilliantly-coloured flowers or leaves. They are known as the shot plants from their habit of bursting their flower buds unexpectedly and releasing pollen. The flowers are insignificant, and the leaves are delicate and finely divided, rather fern-like in appearance.

**Species cultivated** *P. microphylla* (syn. *P. muscosa*), artillery plant, gunpowder plant, pistol plant, 3–15 inches, tropical America; the common names refer to the cloud of pollen which is released when the plant is shaken. *P. nummularifolia,* prostrate, small round leaves, good for hanging baskets, South America. *P. spruceana,* 3–12 inches, dark bronze-green leaves, Peru, Venezuela.

**Cultivation** A compost mixture of loam, leafmould and coarse sand in equal parts suits these plants and small pots of 4–5 inches are used, the plants being put in a lightly shaded position in the house. Potting is carried out from February to April, and the plants watered freely from April to September. The temperature should be 55–65°F (13–18°C) from September to March, and 70–80°F (21–27°C) from March to September. Propagation is by dividing plants between February and March, by taking cuttings from January to May and placing them in small pots in sandy soil in a temperature of 65–75°F (18–24°C), or by sowing seed in spring in sandy soil and placing it in a similar temperature.

## Platycerium (plat-ee-seer-ee-um)

From the Greek *platys,* broad, and *keras,* a horn, in allusion to the broad and horn-shaped fronds *(Polypodiaceae).* Stag's-horn fern. Of this genus of 17 species of ferns several are cultivated in the greenhouse and the stovehouse where, suspended in a moist atmosphere, they are among the strangest-looking of cultivated plants. In nature they grow as epiphytes upon forest trees or clinging to the face of a vertical rock. The fronds are of two distinct kinds. The sterile fronds, known as mantle fronds, are erect and clinging and in nature are pressed against the rock or tree and serve to support the whole plant and also to collect a store of humus from fallen and decaying leaves. The much-branched pendent fronds, which give the plants their common name, are the chief food-assimilating organs. The species most commonly grown is the Australian *P. alcicorne* (syn. *P. bifurcatum*). Some years ago a huge specimen of *P. alcicorne* in a greenhouse at the Royal Horticultural Society's Garden, Wisley, broke

away from its supporting wires and crashed into a water tank beneath, from which it was rescued none the worse for its total immersion. They are decidedly not delicate or flimsy plants.

**Cultivation** The plants, with some fibrous peat and sphagnum moss, are secured by copper wire to blocks of wood, and then suspended. They will grow downwards and sideways, as well as upwards, and quickly become very attractive. *P. bifurcatum* is sometimes used as a house plant, when it is grown in a pot containing sphagnum moss and coarse peat in equal parts. The soil mixture should be kept fairly dry in cold weather, but from spring to autumn, when the fronds droop, the pots may be placed in a bucket of water for a while, until they become rigid again. Otherwise, they may be grown in heated conservatories wired to blocks of wood as described above. Water generously from April to September, but moderately from September to March. Syringe the plants

frequently during the summer. Maintain a temperature of 55–65°F (13–18°C) from October to March, and 70–80°F (21–27°C) from March to October. Propagation is by division or by suckers removed and potted in February or March, or by spores sown on sandy peat in a temperature of 75–85°F (24–30°C).

## Pteris (ter-is)

From the Greek *pteron,* a wing, in allusion to the form of the fronds *(Polypodiaceae* or *Pteridaceae).* This genus of over 250 species of ferns is widespread throughout the world. It once contained hardy as well as tropical ferns, but the former have been transferred to *Pteridium,* including the ubiquitous bracken.

**Greenhouse species cultivated** *P. cretica,* fronds 6–12 inches; vars. *albo-lineata,* long narrow fronds with white centre line; *mayi,* variegated; *wimsettii,* fronds 1½–2 feet long, chestnut-striped. *P. longifolia,* fronds 1–2 feet, tropics and

1 Pilea cadierei, with silvery markings on its dark-green leaves, makes an attractive and particularly unusual plant for the home.
2 The narrow fronds of Pteris argutica ensiformis are silvery green. The plant is a native of the Iberian peninsula, being particularly found in Portugal.
3 Pteris cretica childsii, a fern for the cool greenhouse, has finger-like fronds.
4 The Stag's Horn Fern, Platycerium, here growing in a natural African habitat. Note the sterile mantle fronds holding the plant to the tree (also for feeding) and the erect fertile fronds bearing masses of brown spores.

Japan. *P. multifida* (syn. *P. serrulata*), spider fern, fronds 9–18 inches long, China; there is a crested form. *P. tremula,* Australian brake, fronds 2–4 feet, Australia, New Zealand; vars. *kingiana,* a crested form; *variegata,* silver line in centre of fronds.
**Stovehouse species cultivated** *P. biaurita argyrae,* fronds 6–12 inches, with white line down centre; vars. *quadriaurita,* fronds to 3 feet; *tricolor,* fronds green, white and red.

**Cultivation** A soil mixture consisting of equal parts of loam, leafmould, peat and sand suits these ferns, which may be grown in pots or rock beds or grown in soil beds. They must all be shaded from direct sunlight. Water ·abundantly in spring and summer, but moderately only after this. The temperature for the stove species should be from March to September, 70–80°F (21–27°C), and from September to March, 60–70°F (16–21°C). The greenhouse species require a temperature of 55–65°F (13–18°C), from March to September, and 50–55°F (10–13°C) September to March. Propagation is by spores sown in fine sandy peat in well-drained pans in a temperature of 80°F (27°C) at any time of the year.

### Rhipsalis (rip-sa-lis)

From the Greek *rhips,* a willow or wicker work, in reference to the slender interlacing branches *(Cactaceae).* A genus of about 60 species, greenhouse succulent perennials, mainly epiphytic and growing in nature in forests where there is considerable humidity and plenty of moisture. They are found in tropical America, the West Indies, East and West Africa and Ceylon. Many grow in the forks of trees where there may be plenty of decaying leaves and bird manure.

**1 Pteris quadriaurita argyraea.**
**2 Rhipsalis rosea 'Electra'.**
**3 Rhipsalis warmingiana.**
**4 Rhipsalis prismatica, an epiphytic plant, has slender, much branched, stems.**

**Species cultivated** *R. cassutha,* a hanging bush, flowers small greenish-white or cream, Brazil and tropical Africa. *R. cereuscula,* mistletoe cactus, well-branched stems, flowers white with a yellow stripe, small white berries, Brazil. *R. crispata,* wide flat stems with wavy margins, flowers pale yellow, Brazil. *R. grandiflora,* cylindrical stems, flowers small, greenish-white, Brazil. *R. houlletiana,* pale green flat stems, toothed along the margins, flowers cream, Brazil. *R. paradoxa,* stems triangular in cross-section, each joint twisted in relation to the next so that an angle is above and below a flat side, flowers white, Brazil.
**Cultivation** These plants require a compost richer than that needed by most cacti, consisting of 4 parts of loam, 2 parts of peat and 2 parts of sharp sand. To 1 bushel of this mixture add 1 ounce of ground chalk and 8 ounces of John Innes base fertiliser. The plants must not have too sunny a position in the greenhouse, and the soil should not be kept

dry in warm weather. Water freely from March to September but once a month only between September and March. The temperature in winter should be not less than 45°F (7°C), and in summer the plants can be put out of doors in partial shade. Propagation is by seed sown in John Innes seed compost in pans at a temperature of 70°F (21°C), or by stem cuttings rooted in sharp sand and peat.

## Rhododendron (ro-do-den-dron)

From the Greek *rhodon*, rose, and *dendron*, tree. Possibly the first true rhododendron to be so named was *R. ferrugineum*, the alpenrose, or *rose des alpes (Ericaceae)*. This is a large genus, with up to 600 species, ranging from prostrate alpine plants to tree-like specimens, some with enormous leaves. It includes those plants which were at one time described under the genus *Azalea* and others which were once included in the genus *Rhodora*. There are both evergreen and deciduous species and hybrids. One point which they have in common is that they will not tolerate lime in the soil with only very few exceptions.

Azaleas make most decorative plants when grown in a tub, large Provence pot or fibre-glass container (beware of cement containers because of the lime content) on a terrace, or a patio or in a cold greenhouse. The container must have a layer of crocks over the drainage holes in the bottom. Use a compost consisting of equal parts of a lime-free loam and moist peat, to 2 parts of leaf soil, 1 part of old farmyard manure and 1 part of coarse silver sand to assist drainage. The compost must never be allowed to dry out or the azalea will soon show signs of distress. In such containers they may be grown in districts where the soil is chalky or limy, but they must be watered with rainwater if the tap water is normally 'hard', otherwise they will soon look sickly.

*Tender azaleas* The winter-flowering, pot-grown, azaleas—so-called *A. indica* —make admirable house plants if they can be grown in a room with a moderate temperature and not placed near a radiator where the atmosphere would be far too hot and dry. Use a similar compost to that recommended for other azaleas and spray the plants overhead with tepid water when in the bud stage, otherwise the buds may shrivel and not develop. After flowering, the plants should be kept in a cool place and in mid-May they can be planted out, or the pots plunged, in the open garden in a partially shaded place for the summer. In September the plants should be lifted, repotted and placed in a cool, but sunny room or greenhouse. In November give warmer conditions, about 60°F (16°C), to bring the plants gently along into flower.

Propagation by seed is a ready means of increase. In fact self-sown seedlings appear frequently among established plants. Sow the seed thinly in a pan or box on the surface of sandy peat from mid-January to mid-February and cover it with only a light sprinkling of silver sand. Place in a temperature of about 60°F (16°C) and keep moderately moist. Freshly harvested seed may germinate within a matter of days. Cuttings of firm shoots, about 3 inches long, taken with

1 Azalea, the variety of rhododendron which is commonly grown as a house plant. They are excellent indoors if they can be grown in a room with a moderate temperature but must be kept well away from radiators, where the atmosphere would be too hot and dry.
2 Rhoeo discolor variegata has leaves of a striking colour and produces side rosettes in the axils.

a heel, should be inserted in sandy soil in a propagating frame from June to November with a temperature of about 50 F (10 C). Hormone rooting compounds may be used if desired and mist propagation is useful for rooting azalea cuttings. Layering is an easy method which may be carried out at almost any time of the year, although the early spring is probably the best period to do this. Grafting is done by nurserymen, usually from January to March, in warm

greenhouse conditions. By doing the work early in the year once the stock and scion are united the plant has the remainder of the summer to make growth before the winter.

## Rhoeo (row-ee-oh)

The derivation of this generic name has never been satisfactorily explained since the British botanist H. F. Hance (1827–1886) who named it gave no account of its meaning *(Commelinaceae)*. It is a genus of a single species from Central America and the West Indies. It is much used as a house plant. The species is *R. discolor,* an evergreen plant with erect linear leaves up to 1 foot long and about 2 inches across. They are dark green on the upper surface and purplish below. The variety *vittata* has the leaves longitudinally striped with cream. The flowers are inconspicuous and are produced in small, purple, boat-like containers at the base of the leaves. As the

stem elongates, it produces side rosettes which can be detached and rooted for propagation purposes.

**Cultivation** Either John Innes composts or soilless composts will suit this plant. The winter temperature should be 50°F (10°C), but lower temperatures will do no harm, provided the soil is kept on the dry side. Plants that are cold and wet are liable to rot. During the winter they should receive all the light available, but require moderate shading during the spring and summer. In the home they should be in a well-lit situation, but in one that does not receive much direct sunlight. They like a rather moist atmosphere and this seems of more importance than much water around their roots, although they require normal watering. Once they are in 5-inch pots they will not require further potting on, but will do better if they are given liquid feeds at three-weekly intervals between mid-May and mid-August. Propagation is by cuttings of the offshoots which form at the base of the stems of mature plants.

**Rhoicissus** (roy-siss-us)
From the Greek *rhoia*, a pomegranate, and *kissos*, a vine. The connection with a pomegranate is hard to understand (*Vitaceae* or now, more correctly, *Vitidaceae*). A genus of about 12 species of evergreen climbers from tropical Africa and South Africa. It is doubtful if any species are in cultivation, but one very popular house plant is sold under this name. This is *R. rhomboidea*, a plant which is probably incorrectly named, the plant sold as this being probably the West Indian *Cissus rhombifolia*. It is a moderately vigorous tendrilled climber with trifoliate leaves (the specific name, *rhomboidea*, refers to the simple leaf). The leaflets are rhomboid in shape, the central one being some 5 inches long

but the darkest situations and are tolerant of gas and oil fumes. In the greenhouse they will require some shading during the summer. A moderately moist atmosphere should be maintained during the spring and summer, while during the winter the soil should be kept very much on the dry side. Plants can be potted on annually in spring or every other year, but should be fed at fortnightly intervals during the summer in the years in which they are not potted on. The growing points are usually nipped out in April and in June to encourage the formation of a bushy specimen and they must also be given some support up which they can climb. Propagation is by cuttings of firm young growths, which will root easily, especially if they are given a little bottom heat. Apart from stopping, pruning is unnecessary unless the plant becomes too large, when it can be cut back very hard in early spring.

### Rochea (ro-she-a)
Commemorating the early nineteenth-century French botanical writer, François de la Roche (Crassulaceae). A genus of four species of greenhouse succulent plants from South Africa. They are semi-shrubby, with leaves occurring in pairs, and the flowers developing at the tips of the shoots. They make good house plants.

**Species cultivated** R. coccinea, 20 inches, leaves thickly produced in four ranks, up to 1 inch long, flowers bright red, produced in profusion, July. R. odoratissima, erect shoots, loosely leaved, flowers pink. R. versicolor, 2-feet thick fleshy stems, with many dark green leaves, flowers white, pink, yellow or bright red, spring.

**Cultivation** The soil mixture should consist of John Innes potting compost No 3 with $\frac{1}{6}$ part added of coarse sand, grit or broken brick. Frequent repotting will be necessary. In winter a minimum temperature of 45°F (7°C) should be maintained, and only sufficient water given to prevent undue shrivelling of the leaves. In summer any bright sunny position is satisfactory and water can be freely given. These plants do well planted in the open garden on a well-drained site during summer when the leaves will turn bright red. The flowers are freely carried in spring and early summer. Propagation is mainly by stem cuttings taken at any time during the growing period and rooted in a mixture of coarse sand and peat. These plants have been freely hybridised for the florist's potted-plant trade and are available in several flower colours.

### Saintpaulia (pronounced in England as written, but san-pole-ee-er elsewhere)
Named in honour of Baron von Saint-Paul-Illaire (1860–1910), who discovered S. ionantha in 1892 (Gesneriaceae). A genus of about 12 species, one only of

and 3 inches across, while the two lateral leaflets are about an inch less in length and width. The young growth is covered with brownish hairs, which soon fall, leaving dark green, glabrous leaves. R. rhomboidea is a native of Natal. A selected form has been given the name 'Jubilee'.

**Cultivation** A compost such as John Innes No 2 or 3 will prove very suitable for these plants. They require a winter temperature of 50 F (10°C) and will relish heat during their growing period. In the home they appear to thrive in all

**1** The long leaves of Rhoeo discolor are dark green on the upper surface and purplish beneath.
**2** The plant commonly known as Rhoicissus rhomboidea is an evergreen climber used as a house plant.
**3** Rocheas, with their bright flowers, are grown as greenhouse succulents and sometimes as pot plants indoors. Rochea subulata has white flowers.
**4** Rochea coccinea flowers in early summer with bright red blooms carried at the top of a stem covered in four-ranked leaves.

which is in general cultivation. This is *S. ionantha,* the popular African violet which is much cultivated in rooms as well as in greenhouses. It is a dwarf plant with dark green, hairy, heart-shaped leaves about 2 inches long borne on reddish stalks about 4 inches long. The flowers of the wild plant are dark violet with yellow anthers, but numerous cultivars have been selected to give plants with white, pink, reddish-purple and lavender flowers. There are also some double-flowered cultivars. The flowers are borne in few-flowered cymes. Some cultivars have leaves that are a paler green than normal and these may be lobed.

The plants flower practically without stopping in the greenhouse and about three times a year in dwelling rooms. In the wild it is a native of Tanzania.

**Cultivation** The plants like a light soil mixture and that generally used is composed of 3 parts of peat, 1 part of loam and 1 part of sharp sand. The plants could be expected to do well in soilless composts. Saintpaulias have a small root system only and rarely require to go beyond a 5-inch pot. For this plant plastic pots have been found to be more satisfactory than clay pots. The other requisites for the plants are shade, warmth and a moist atmosphere. This latter is not easy to provide in dwellings and it is best either to stand the pot on pebbles, which are standing in water in such a way that the base of the pot is clear of the water, but so that the vapour can ascend round the plant as the water evaporates, or to plunge the pot in another container, filling the interstices with some water-retentive medium such as peat, moss, sand or vermiculite. This is kept moist at all times. The plants themselves do not take great quantities of water, but this should always be given at the same temperature. The best temperature appears to be 60°F (16°C) but provided it is not too cold or too warm, the exact temperature does not seem to matter as much as seeing that this temperature is always maintained. Waterings where the temperature fluctuates will cause the appearance of unsightly white blotches on the leaves. The temperature should ideally be 55°F (13°C) at night, and 70°F (21°C) during the daytime, and if this can be kept going throughout the year the plants will do particularly well. However, this is not always possible and lower readings will slow down growth, but will not cause any damage, provided that the temperature does not fall for long below 50°F (10°C). When temperatures are low the soil should be kept rather dry and the atmosphere should also not be too moist. In dwellings this will occur automatically as the water will evaporate more slowly, but in greenhouses this means that the house should not be damped down too frequently. Established

plants should be given weak feeds at fortnightly intervals between April and October. Between November and mid-February no shading is necessary, but after this date the sun may get rather fierce and light shading should be supplied which will require intensifying at the end of April. This is a good time for doing any potting on that may be necessary.

Propagation is by seed or by leaf-cuttings. The seed is very fine and should be placed on the surface of the pot, which is then encased in a polythene bag. A temperature of 70°F (21°C) is necessary to ensure germination. The seed should be sown as early in the year as is possible, having regard to the temperature needed. The seedlings are subsequently pricked out and potted up. The various cultivars must be propagated by leaf cuttings. A leaf is taken with its stalk and the end is inserted shallowly in the propagating medium. Under warm conditions a number of plantlets will form at the base. As soon as they are large enough to handle, these plantlets should be separated and pricked out and then potted up individually when large enough. The young plants should not be allowed to flower until they are of a good size, otherwise they become weakened and never become really healthy.

1 and 2 The large flowers of 'Diana'
hybrids of Saintpaulia ionantha may be
in varying shades of pink or mauve.
3 Sansevieria hahnii variegata is grown
as a pot plant for indoor decoration.
4 and 5 Sansevieria trifasciata laurentii
which grows naturally in South Africa
and prefers light situations elsewhere.

**Sansevieria** (san-sev-ee-air-ee-a)
Commemorating Raimond de Sansgrio
or Sangro (1710–71), who was Prince of
Sansevierio *(Liliaceae)*. Angola hemp,
bowstring hemp. According to modern
botanists the generic name should be
*Sanseverinia*. A genus of 60 species of
rhizomatous perennials, natives of
Arabia, tropical and South Africa, and
Madagascar, with very thick leathery
leaves and rather inconspicuous white
or greenish flowers, not often seen in
cultivation except, perhaps, in warm
greenhouses or stovehouses. Those in
cultivation are grown for the sake of
their leaves. S. hahnii and S. trifasciata
are popular house plants.
**Species cultivated** S. cylindrica, leaves
cylindrical, 1 inch thick, up to 3 feet long
in mature specimens, flowers whitish on
a 2-foot stem; the raceme can be 2 feet
long, August, tropical Africa. S. grandis,
leaves to 3 feet long, 6 inches across, dull
green with darker bands, flowers white
in panicles, tropical Africa. S. hahnii,
leaves in a rosette, about 6 inches long,
4 inches across, obovate with a slender
point, dark green, mottled with very

light horizontal bands, tropical Africa.
*S. trifasciata,* leaves erect, sword-
shaped, slightly waved at the edge,
usually about 18 inches high and 2
inches across, dark green with transverse
bands of lighter green; var. *laurentii,* is
the one most frequently seen, it has a
golden margin to the leaves, western
tropical Africa.
**Cultivation** A compost such as John
Innes or one composed of 2 parts of loam
to 1 of leafmould and ¾ part of sharp
sand is necessary for these plants. With
their leathery leaves they are tolerant of
long periods of drought and, though they
prefer a winter temperature of 50°F
(10°C), they will tolerate lower temperatures if the soil is kept very dry. Even
during the summer they will take less
water than most plants. In the home S.
hahnii and S. trifasciata will do best in
a well-lit situation, but will survive in
shady positions. In the greenhouse all
species require shading in the summer,
but full light at other times. Potting on
is best done in April or early May.
Propagation is by careful division or by
leaf cuttings. A leaf cutting of the
variegated forms will give rise to
unvariegated plants and so these must
be propagated by division. It is some
time before roots form at the base of the
new leaves and they must not be
separated before they are at least 8
inches high. If the rhizome can be cut
half through when they are 6 inches
high, it will hasten rooting.

**Schefflera** (she-fler-a)
Commemorating J. C. Scheffler of Danzig *(Araliaceae)*. A genus of 200 species of shrubs and small trees from tropical and sub-tropical parts of the world.

**Species cultivated** *S. actinophylla* (E), umbrella tree, to 25 feet in nature, leaves to 1 foot across, deeply lobed, leaflets five (three in young plants), glossy green, flowers red, in panicles to 4 feet long, though it is uncertain whether it has flowered in cultivation, Australia, Java. *S. digitata* (E), shrub or tree, to 25 feet in nature, leaves deeply digitate, flowers greenish in panicles as much as 1 foot long, New Zealand.

**Cultivation** A large pot or the greenhouse border should be chosen for these plants which are grown for their foliage effect, and the soil mixture should consist of equal parts of loam, peat and coarse sand. Plant in spring or autumn. Maintain a minimum winter temperature of 45–50°F (7–10°C), water freely from spring to autumn, but moderately only in winter, especially when temperatures are low. Propagation is easily managed by rooting cuttings of ripe growth in a propagating frame in spring, or under a frame in summer. *S. actinophylla* makes a good house plant, requiring little heat to keep it in good condition.

**Schizanthus** (skiz-an-thus; shy-zan-thus)
From the Greek *schizo,* to cut, and *anthos,* flower, in reference to the deeply cut corolla *(Solanaceae)*. A genus of 15 species of showy and attractive annual plants from Chile, sometimes known as the butterfly flowers, or the poor man's orchids. They are suitable for cold greenhouse cultivation, or can be sown in heat and bedded out in late spring or early summer.

**Species cultivated** *S. grahamii,* 2 feet, lilac, rose and yellow, June to October. *S. pinnatus,* 2 feet, violet and yellow, but may be other colours, June to October. *S. retusus,* 2½ feet, rose and orange, July to September. *S. × wisetonensis,* hybrid of first two species, combines their characteristics. Garden strains which have evolved from hybridising include: 'Danbury Park Strain', pansy-flowered, pink, crimson, purple and white; 'Dr Badger's Hybrids Improved', large flowers, colours ranging from white and yellow through lilac and rose; 'Dwarf Bouquet', bright rose, crimson, salmon, amber, and pink; Wisetonensis 'Monarch Signal', feathery leaves, cherry red orchid-like flowers.

**Cultivation** Schizanthus are usually grown as cold greenhouse plants and provide a most attractive display in late winter and early spring. Sow the seeds in August in John Innes seed compost, in a frame or cool greenhouse, and transplant the seedlings when large enough to handle, to 3-inch pots containing John Innes potting compost No 1, giving them as much light as possible, and a temperature of 45–55°F (7–13°C) until January. Then put them in 6-inch pots and grow them in a light position, but do not allow them to become pot-bound. Stop the plants frequently to keep them bushy, and support them by tying them to stakes. In winter they should be moderately watered, but freely at other times, and they benefit from the application of liquid fertilisers occasionally while flowering.

When grown as half-hardy annuals for planting out of doors, seed is sown under glass in February–March in a temperature of 65–75°F (18–24°C). The seedlings are pricked off when they are about 1 inch high, and then planted out in May after being hardened off. They can also be sown where they are required to grow, in May, but require a warm sheltered site if this is to be done; they will then flower in August.

1

## Schlumbergera (schlum-ber-ger-a)

Commemorating F. Schlumberger, owner of a famous plant collection *(Cactaceae)*. A genus of a few species of succulent perennials, suitable for the greenhouse or sunny window. The plants are rather similar in form to *Zygocactus,* but the stems are a darker green and stouter, with pronounced notches on the sides of the stems. The flowers appear in spring from areoles at the tips of the joints, and are very freely produced.

**Species cultivated** *S. gaertneri,* Easter cactus, very free-flowering even on small plants, flat, deeply notched stems, flowers bright scarlet, April–May, Brazil. *S. russelliana,* violet-pink, spring, Brazil.

**Cultivation** John Innes potting compost No 2 is suitable, with added roughage if the soil is not porous enough. Repot after flowering each year, and keep shaded in summer whether in a greenhouse or out of doors. Water freely from the beginning of March to September, otherwise once a fortnight will be sufficient. The winter temperature should be not less than 50°F (10°C), rising to about 65°F (18°C) between March and September. Plants are easily propagated from cuttings of short pieces of stem, rooted in equal parts of coarse sand and peat. Spray the cuttings every other day or so and pot them up when the roots have formed. They may also be propagated by grafting on to *Pereskia,* or any other upright stock, to form an 'umbrella' type of plant.

## Scindapsus (skin-dap-sus)

The name is taken from *skindapsos,* the ancient Greek name for an ivy-like plant *(Araceae).* A genus of 40 species of climbing stovehouse shrubs from eastern Asia, of which a few are cultivated for the decorative value of their evergreen leaves. The arum-like flowers are rarely produced in cultivation. They are related to *Caladium. S. aureus* and its cultivars, and *S. pictus argyraeus* are sold as house plants.

**Species cultivated** *S. aureus,* 20 feet, leaves blotched with yellow, to 1½ feet long, Solomon Islands; 'Giant Leaf' is a cultivar in which mature leaves, three times the size of juvenile leaves, are produced when the plant is still young; 'Golden Queen' is a cultivar with yellow leaves; 'Marble Queen' has white leaves netted with green. *S. officinalis,* to 4 feet, leaves to 10 inches, India. *S. pictus,* silver vine, 40 feet, leaves glaucous with darker spots, East Indies; var. *argyraeus,* juvenile form, leaves olive-green with silver spots.

**Cultivation** A soil mixture of equal parts of rough peat, sphagnum moss and coarse potting sand with charcoal is needed, and potting should be done in February or March. It looks well to have these climbers attached to such things as the trunks of tree ferns or other substantial supports. Water copiously from March to October and then moderately during winter. Spray overhead at all seasons. Give a temperature from September to March of 60–65°F (16–18°C), and March to September, 80–85°F (27–30°C). Shade from direct sunlight. Propagation is by division of roots at potting time, or by cuttings rooted in a propagating case with bottom heat. When grown as house plants less water is required and plants should never be over-watered. They require a reasonably light position, but not one in full sun.

## Spathiphyllum (spa-thi-fil-um)

From the Greek *spatha,* spathe, and *phyllon,* leaf, in reference to the leaf-like spathe *(Araceae).* A genus of small evergreen perennials with predominantly white and green spathes. Most of them require stovehouse conditions, though *S. wallisii* is grown as a house plant. There are 36 species, natives of Central America and South America, the Philippines, Celebes, Molucca.

**Cultivation** These plants should always be grown in a humid atmosphere and with frequent use of the syringe. The temperature should be kept between 65 and 70 F (18 and 21 C) from September to March, and 75–85 F (24–30 C) from March to September. They grow best in a compost of leafmould and peat with a little charcoal, sand and loam. Propagation is by division in February or March, or by seeds sown in a temperature of 85 F (30 C) during February.

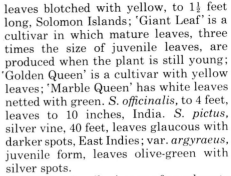

1 The showy hybrid Schizanthus, Butterfly Flower or Poor Man's Orchid, makes a colourful display in the greenhouse in spring from an autumn sowing.
2 Scindapsus aureus, a climbing stovehouse shrub with yellow-blotched leaves which may reach up to 18 inches. When grown as a house-plant Scindapsus should never be over-watered and should be placed in a reasonably light position but not in full sun.

*S. wallisii,* is commonly grown as a house plant. It needs a good deal of care to cultivate it successfully but is one of the few such plants grown for its flowers. These are green at first, then white, finally turning green again, the whole process lasting a month or more and taking place twice a year, in spring and autumn. The plant needs constant shade, frequent feeding and regular repotting, as it grows rapidly.

## Stenocarpus (sten-o-car-pus)

From the Greek *stenos,* narrow, and *karpos,* fruit, referring to the fruits *(Proteaceae).* A genus of 25 species of trees which are somewhat slender and attain a height of from 20–100 feet, with handsome foliage and attractive flowers followed by narrow fruits several inches long containing many densely packed, winged seeds. They come from eastern Australia and New Caledonia; the two species discussed are both natives of Australia.

**Species cultivated** *S. salignus,* 20–50 feet, flowers yellowish, fragrant, borne in umbels with 10–20 and sometimes as many as 30 flowers in each umbel if the tree is growing really well. *S. sinuatus,* tulip flower or fire-wheel tree, 30–100 feet, leaves undivided or deeply pinnately lobed, 12–18 inches long, reddish underneath, flowers bright red, borne in umbels of 12–20 on stalks ½ inch long radiating from the top of the peduncle like the spokes of a wheel from a central hub.

**Cultivation** Both species are suitable for cultivation in the cool conservatory and are probably hardy in the very mild localities of Britain. *S. sinuatus* is, however, the more spectacular in flower and has the advantage that it will flower when only quite small. Propagation is either by seed or vegetatively; better results are obtained by air layering than by stem cuttings.

## Streptocarpus (Strep-toe-karp-us)

From the Greek *streptos,* twisted, and *karpos,* fruit; the seed capsules are twisted into a spiral *(Gesneriaceae).* A genus of 100 species of tropical herbs, mainly natives of tropical and subtropical Africa, grown for their showy tubular flowers. The genus is divided into two subgenera. Plants with a main stem and stalked leaves in opposite pairs belong to the subgenus *Streptocarpella* and are rarely cultivated. In the subgenus *Streptocarpus* the leaves spring directly from the rootstock. The various species are now rather rare in cultivation, but a hybrid strain is among the most popular of greenhouse plants.

**Species cultivated** *S.* × *hybridus,* many parents have entered into this strain but the two most important are the single-leaved, brick-red *S. dunnii* and the variable *S. rexii* (see below). The plants have the leaves in rosettes; the leaves are wrinkled and about 6 inches long.

The flower scapes are about 9 inches long and bear usually about 5 flowers. These are tubular with an extended limb, up to 2 inches long and about as much across. They are in varying shades of pink, purple, blue, violet and white, sometimes with pencilling in the throat, and they flower throughout the summer. *S. rexii,* leaves up to 10 inches long, in a rosette, flower stems about 6 inches long and bearing one or two flowers only, which may be white, bluish or violet-mauve and are about 1½ inches long with purple stripes on the lower lip, Cape Province. *S. wendlandii,* the plant carries only a single ovate leaf, which may be up to 2½ feet long and 2 feet across, the underside is reddish-purple, while the upper surface has a purplish tinge, flowers violet, about 2 inches long and 1½ inches across, borne on a many-flowered scape (up to 30 flowers have been recorded) about 1 foot high, Natal.

**Cultivation** Streptocarpus are generally treated as greenhouse annuals and so loamless composts will suit them well, although they will also thrive in the John Innes mixtures. The seed is very fine and should be placed on the surface of the soil and the pot covered with a pane of glass or enveloped in a polythene bag. A temperature of at least 65 F (18 C) should be provided. Seed can be sown at any time in the late winter or spring when such temperatures are easily provided. As soon as the seedlings are large enough to handle they are pricked out into boxes, then potted into 3-inch pots and finally into 5-inch pots, although it is possible to pot on still further. *S.* × *hybridus* and *S. rexii* will flower in four months, but *S. wendlandii* may not flower until the second year. The plants like a warm, moist atmosphere and to be shaded from very bright sunshine, but they should also be given plenty of air. They will take ample water while making their growth, but if they are to be over-wintered they should then be kept on the dry side. A temperature of 50 F (10 C) is satisfactory for over-wintering. *S. wendlandii* is sometimes monocarpic and dies after flowering, but this is not invariable. Apart from seed, plants can be propagated by means of leaf cuttings. The leaves are scored with a knife on the underside and laid on the propagating medium, much as is done with Rex begonias. If plants are over-wintered and can be given some heat in the spring they can be got into flower much earlier in the year. Plants that are to be kept for more than one year are probably better grown in John

1 The Fire-wheel Tree, Stenocarpus sinuatus, a native of Australia.
2, 3 and 4 Streptocarpus hybrids are in various shades of pink, blue, mauve and white, sometimes pencilled.
5 Streptocarpus 'Constant Nymph'. Streptocarpus like a warm moist atmosphere and should be shaded from very bright sunshine. They should be given plenty of air and fed with ample water during growth. Over the winter period, however, they should be kept at 10°C (50°F) and rather dry.

Innes potting compost.

## Tetrastigma (tet-ra-stig-ma)
From the Greek *tetra,* four, and stigma: the stigma is four-lobed *(Vitaceae).* Related to *Cissus* and *Vitis,* these are vigorous tendril-climbing plants with digitate leaves, containing about 90 species. The genus is found in tropical or subtropical Asia, Indo-Malaysia and Australia. One species only is commonly cultivated, *T. voinierianum,* a vigorous, evergreen climber, eventually capable of spreading 20 feet or so, but not a very rapid grower. The mature leaf, consisting of five leaflets, may be 8 inches long and 10 inches wide, while each leaflet may be 6 inches long and 4 inches wide. They are a soft green when mature, but covered with a silvery-grey indumentum as they unfurl. The plant comes from Vietnam, and was at one time much used as a house plant, but is rather large for most dwellings.

**Cultivation** John Innes potting compost is perfectly suitable, but better results have been obtained with a compost of 2 parts of light loam, 1½ parts of leaf-mould, 1 part of sand, 1 part of rotted dung and ½ part of peat. To every barrow load of this mixture a 5-inch potful of superphosphate and a similar amount of bonemeal should be added. Larger specimens can be obtained by

planting out in the greenhouse border. The winter temperature should be 55°F (13°C), but the plant will come to little harm at 50°F (10°C). During the summer a moist atmosphere should be maintained, but the plants are kept as dry as possible during the winter. The young growing shoots are very brittle and should be supported. Potting on is best done in late March, but once in an 8-inch or 9-inch pot the plants should be left there and the top 3 inches of compost renewed yearly, while liquid feeds should be applied at three-weekly intervals between mid-May and mid-August. The plants can be shaded quite heavily during the period from May to mid-August. In the home they should be placed in a situation that is well-lit, but which does not receive much direct sunlight. A moist atmosphere is necessary in late spring and summer. Fresh air should be admitted when the temperature exceeds 70°F (21°C). Propagation is by cuttings of firm young growths, which will root quickly in gentle heat.

### Tillandsia (til-land-see-a)
Named in honour of a Swedish botanist, Elias Tillands (1640–1693) *(Bromeliaceae)*. A genus of some 500 species of epiphytic, herbaceous plants of considerable variation in form, found from the southern United States to the Argentine. In the West Indies the unattractive *T. recurvata* will attach itself to telephone wires, and the Spanish moss of the Florida everglades is *T. usneoides*.
**Species cultivated** *T. cyanea,* forms a rosette of long, narrow, rather rush-like grey leaves, to 15 inches long, and 1 inch across at their widest, the inflorescence on a 6-inch stem is, itself, about 4 inches long and wide, consisting of overlapping pink bracts and blue flowers 1½ inches across, summer, Guatemala. *T. lindeniana,* similar, slightly broader leaves with a purple flush, inflorescence on a 6-inch stem is, itself, about 8 inches long, consisting of coral-pink or carmine bracts and blue, white-throated flowers, 2 inches wide, summer, Peru; vars. *luxurians,* several inflorescences; *major,* larger flowers; *regeliana,* green bracts.

*T. usneoides,* Spanish moss, forms long trails with greyish leaves about 2 inches long, flowers minute, yellowish-green, July, tropical America.
**Cultivation** *T. usneoides* should be suspended on some other plant or fastened to a piece of cork bark and given some sphagnum moss to encourage it to attach itself. It requires warm, shady conditions with a winter temperature of 50 F (10 C). The other two species can be planted in a mixture of equal parts of peat, sharp sand and osmunda fibre, or they, too, can be attached to a piece of cork bark with some moist sphagnum moss to encourage the roots to emerge and attach themselves. The centre of the rosette should be filled with rainwater and the osmunda mixture or the sphagnum moss should be kept moist. The plants like ample fresh air and will do best if suspended near the roof of the house, and fresh air should be admitted during the summer as often as possible, although the temperature should not fall below 65 F (18 C) during this time and higher readings are appreciated. The glass should be slightly shaded from mid-June to mid-August, but otherwise the plants appreciate all the light available, unlike *T. usneoides* which requires shady conditions. *T. cyanea* and *T. lindeniana* need a winter temperature of 55 F (13 C), although they will survive at lower temperatures. Any water applied during the winter

should be at a temperature of 55 F (13 C). After flowering the main rosette will probably die, but the side rosettes can be grown on; as the main rosette is dying it should be carefully cut away with a knife before the rhizome rots. The only other form of propagation is by seed, which should be sown in a mixture of leafmould topped with sand at a temperature of 80 F (27 C).

### Tradescantia (trad-es-kan-tee-a)
Commemorating John Tradescant (died 1637), gardener to Charles I *(Commelinaceae)*. A genus of 60 species of hardy perennial and greenhouse plants from North America and tropical South America. The hardy varieties are commonly called spiderwort, flower of a day, Moses-in-the-bulrushes, or devil-in-the-pulpit. According to some botanists the garden plants grown under the name *T. virginiana* belong to a hybrid group known as *T. × andersoniana*.
**Species cultivated** *T. albiflora,* wandering Jew, trailing, fast-growing greenhouse or house plant with shiny stems, swollen at the nodes, leaves narrow, pointed, South America; several variegated forms are known with cream and yellow-striped leaves, green and white, or with faint red markings. *T. blossfeldiana,* creeping or trailing greenhouse or house plant, dark green leathery leaves, purple and whitely-hairy beneath, Argentine. *T. fluminensis,*

wandering Jew, trailing greenhouse or house plant, often confused with *T. albiflora*, leaves slender-pointed, green, purplish-red beneath; several variegated forms, South America. *T. virginiana* (or *T. × andersoniana*) spiderwort, etc., hardy perennial, 1½–2 feet, flowers violet-blue from June to September, eastern United States; vars. *alba*, a white form; *coerulea*, bright blue; 'Iris Prichard', white, shaded violet at the centre; 'J. C. Weguelin', large, azure-blue; 'Osprey', large, white, with feathery blue stamens; *rosea*, pink, *rubra*, dark ruby-red.

**Cultivation** The tender species and varieties require a minimum winter temperature of 55 F (13 C), and should be potted in March or April, in ordinary potting soil. Avoid a rich compost which may cause the leaves to turn green and lose their variegations. Hardy varieties can be grown in ordinary garden soil in sun or partial shade. Lift and divide in autumn or spring every three or four years. Propagation of tender species is by cuttings taken from April to August and inserted in pots of sandy soil in a warm propagating frame; they will root in four to six weeks. Hardy varieties may be increased by division in the spring.

**Vriesea** (vree-zee-a)
Commemorating W. de Vriese, a Dutch

**1 Tillandsia flabellata is notable for its bright red flower bracts.**
**2 Tetrastigma voinierianum is a vigorous and spreading climbing plant with large leaves.**
**3 Tradescantia virginiana is a good herbaceous perennial for damp soil.**
**4 Vriesea splendens, a very popular house plant, has wine-coloured bands on the leaves that disappear once the plant has flowered.**

botanist of the nineteenth century (Bromeliaceae). A genus of some 190 species, mainly epiphytic, from South and Central America, with attractive, handsome unarmed leaves, borne in rosettes, and/or flowers. *V. splendens* is a popular house plant. The generic name is usually, but incorrectly spelt Vriesia.
**Species cultivated** *V. carinata*, leaves 8 inches long, about 1 inch wide, bracts conspicuous, red and yellow, flowers yellow, in a spike about 3 inches long, autumn, Brazil. *V. fenestralis*, leaves handsome, 18 inches long, light green with darker reticulations, bracts green, brown-spotted, flowers tubular, greenish-yellow in a spike to 1½ feet, Brazil. *V. hieroglyphica*, to 5 feet, leaves dark green with bands, black on the upper surface and purple below, bracts dull yellow, flowers yellow in a branched

inflorescence, 3 feet high, Brazil. *V. saundersii* (syn. *Encholirion saundersii*), leaves 10 inches long, grey to green with red blotches at the base, bracts pale yellow, flowers tubular, yellow, in a branched inflorescence, Brazil. *V. splendens*, leaves 12–15 inches long, dark green, with wine-coloured bands until the flowers appear, bracts bright red, flowers yellow in a 15-inch long inflorescence, bracts remain coloured for at least 6 weeks, Guyana. *V. tessellata*, 6 feet, variable plant, leaves 15 inches long, chequered white, yellow and green, Brazil; vars. *roseo-picta*, large pink dots; *sanderae*, white and yellow bands on a chequered green ground.
**Cultivation** A compost of equal parts of peat, sharp sand and osmunda fibre is best for mature plants. The 'vase' in the centre of the rosette should be kept filled with rainwater and this should be warmed to a temperature of 55°F (13°C) in winter. Winter temperatures should be 50°F (10°C) for *V. carinata*, *V. saundersii* and *V. splendens*, 55°F (13°C) for the other species, which require to be shaded from early spring until the end of September. The species that will tolerate cooler conditions will also appreciate more light, and no shading need be applied until the end of May. Mature plants should receive fresh air whenever the inside temperature reaches 70°F (21°C). During late spring and summer, very minute quantities of liquid feed can be added to the water in the 'vase' at three-weekly intervals. No harm will be done if the species which will winter at 50°F (10°C) are given the higher temperature that the tessellated-leaved species require. After flowering the adult rosette dies away, when the side-rosettes may be detached and potted up separately in a mixture of equal parts of leafmould, sphagnum moss and peat and rooted with bottom heat of between 70–80°F (21–27°C). They should be heavily shaded. Once rooted, they are gradually hardened off and brought into more light. Propagation by seed is slow and a temperature of 80°F (27°C) is necessary.

### Zebrina (ze-bry-na)

From *zebra*, the Portuguese word—the leaves are striped like a zebra's coat *(Commelinaceae)*. A genus of four or five species of trailing greenhouse perennials, natives of the southern United States to Central America. They are related to the genus *Tradescantia*.

**Species cultivated** *Z. pendula,* wandering Jew, stems creeping, leaves dark green, striped white above, purplish below; var. *quadricolor,* leaves green, striped red and grey. *Z. purpusii* (syn. *Tradescantia purpurea),* pendulous in habit, leaves dull purple above, bright purple below, flowers purplish-pink.

**Cultivation** Zebrinas do well in a compost of equal parts of sand, leafmould and loam. They will grow in baskets suspended from the roof, or in beds under the greenhouse staging. They should be potted or planted between January or April, watered freely from March to October and more moderately afterwards. Maintain a temperature of 40–50 F (4–10 C) from October to April, 55–65 F (13–18 C) from April to October. They should never be exposed to extremes of temperature. Propagation is by cuttings of young shoots inserted in light soil in a propagating frame between March and October.

### Zygocactus (si-go-kak-tus)

From the Greek *zygon*, a yoke, and *Cactus*, possibly referring to the shape of the stem joints *(Cactaceae).* Christmas cactus. A genus of a single species, an epiphytic greenhouse cactus, placed by some botanists as a hybrid in the genus *Schlumbergera.* The species is *Z. truncatus,* from eastern Brazil. It has flat, short stems with small areoles, minute spines and claw-like joints. Cerise-red

Vriesea fenestralis (opposite page) a delightful member of a species which originated in South America. Zygocactus truncatus (above), the Christmas Cactus, is easy to grow and produces these attractive cerise red flowers in winter – when it is at its best.

flowers are freely-produced from the ends of the joints from December to February; vars. *altensteinii,* teeth on stems more pronounced, flowers brick-red; *crenatus,* flowers small, bluish-violet; *delicatus,* growth more erect, flowers pale pink.

**Cultivation** *Z. truncatus* is easy to grow, either on its own roots or grafted on to a tall stock to make an umbrella-shaped specimen. Use John Innes potting compost No 2 with added leafmould. Repot every two years or when the plant becomes too large for its pot, repotting when flowering has ceased. In winter maintain a minimum temperature of 50 F (10 C), increasing this to 60 F (16 C) as buds form. Water when the soil has almost dried out, throughout the winter. In June plants may be placed out of doors in semi-shade. Plants do not like a sunny position in an un-shaded greenhouse; they do better in a medium-lighted room in the house. Give them a weak liquid feed after flowering. When plants are in bud do not move them and at this time, in particular, protect them from draughts. The causes of bud drop are too wet or too dry a soil or a changeable atmosphere. Propagation is by cuttings which are best taken in early summer and rooted in sharp sand, spraying them occasionally. Or plants may be grafted on to *Pereskia* stock.

# Choosing and caring for your plants

Two delightful and popular flowering plants, Fuchsia 'Melody' (opposite page) and Begonia Semperflorens (this page).

There are two kinds of plant that we bring into our houses. The more spectacular are the flowering plants, cyclamen, azaleas or African violets. Unfortunately their season of attractiveness is limited. All too soon the flowers will fade and the plants then have little attraction. If you have a greenhouse, you can keep the plant going and prepare it for another season, but we usually do not feel inclined to keep it in the house; certainly not in a conspicuous position. The other kind of plant is less spectacular; its beauty is centred in its foliage rather than in its flowers, but it has the advantage that, provided you treat it properly, it will grow permanently in your rooms and increase in size and effect from year to year. These plants, grown for permanent effect, are commonly known as house plants.

Most of us do not live in glass houses; therefore the plants we can grow in our rooms are limited in number. Even a room that appears well lit to us, will seem shady to a plant and, as a result, the majority of houseplants are those that can tolerate shade. If a plant is to be permanently attractive, it should be evergreen. We can visualise exceptions, such as the bonsai dwarf trees, where the outline of the tree is attractive even when no leaves are visible, but there are not many of these exceptions to the demand for evergreen plants. Again most of us live in rooms of only moderate size and we require plants of moderate dimensions. We also do not want them to grow too quickly. Re-potting is a tedious operation for those who live in flats or in houses without gardens and we do not want to have to undertake it more than once a year at the most. Although plain green leaves are attractive enough, particularly if they have interesting shapes, leaves that contain some colour are usually regarded as more attractive. Colour in leaves occurs in two forms. Some leaves are naturally coloured; for instance those of Rex begonias and *Cordyline terminalis,* but there are other plants which produce coloured forms of their normally green leaves. These are described as variegated and the variegation may be due to a number of causes. Seeds, in fact, are very unlikely to transmit variegation. Not everyone finds variegated leaves attractive but many do and, as a result, many plants are popular because of their variegated leaves that would otherwise be little regarded. The popular variegated forms of *Tradescantia fluviatilis* and *Chlorophytum capense* may be cited as examples. With half or more of the chlorophyll lacking, the leaves of variegated plants can only do half the work of normal green leaves and so variegated plants tend to grow more slowly than the unvariegated forms. This is not unexpected; a more surprising result of variegation, though it is not always the case, is that the plants are often more tender than the normal forms. There seems to be no very obvious explanation for this.

We can now summarise the qualities that we require for a house plant. It must be compact in habit of growth, tolerant of shade and evergreen. The leaves should be attractive, either by reason of their shape or their colour: if we can have attractive flowers as well, so much the better, but with the emphasis to be laid on the permanence of the attraction, agreeable flowers are obviously a bonus. In fact the combination of handsome flowers and handsome leaves is somewhat rare in any branch of gardening. Among the house plants many of the bromeliads provide an exception to this rule, but even with these plants the showiest part of the inflorescence is due to the coloured bracts that surround the flowers, and these are really modified leaves.

Temperate climates produce few plants with the characteristics that we require. The various ivies form an important exception to this statement, but, even so, the great majority of house plants come from the tropics. Plants are infinitely adaptable, as a general rule (there are, of course, exceptions and these are generally regarded as 'difficult' plants) and most tropical plants will adapt themselves to temperate conditions and even to the fluctuating lengths of daylight, which, even more than the alteration in temperature, mark the chief difference between tropical and temperate climates.

There are certain temperatures, varying from plant to plant, below which plant growth ceases. The plant may

**House plants (left) group attractively. A Fuchsia (right) called 'Dutch Mill.'**

survive perfectly well, but it will neither produce fresh roots nor fresh leaves, until the temperature is raised. It is, obviously, more difficult to produce high temperatures when the outside temperature is very low and so it is most convenient to make our winter the equivalent of the tropical plant's dry season. The dry season in the tropics is generally very hot, but, owing to the lack of water, the plant makes no growth and stays in a dormant condition. This is one of the reasons why all house plant growers are recommended to keep their plants as dry as possible during the winter. How dry you can keep them, will depend on the type of plant you are growing and on how warm you keep your rooms.

The type of heating that you use and the temperatures you maintain in your various rooms during the winter will affect the types of plant you can grow. Some plants, notably begonias, are very intolerant of gas fumes, so that if your rooms are heated by gas, you will not be able to grow begonias satisfactorily. If you have really warm rooms, maintaining, perhaps, an average temperature of 70 F (21 C), they will be far too warm for such plants as ivy or x *Fatshedera lizei*. With high temperatures such as these, the plants will continue growing during the winter and more water will be required. The winter growth may not be very ornamental, as the lack of light will prevent the formation of good sized leaves.

## The right temperature

Many house plants are 'stopped' in the spring: that is to say that the tips of the various shoots are nipped out, so as to induce the formation of secondary shoots that will give the plant a nice bushy appearance, and where this is done the weak winter growth can be removed. However, there are plants, such as most of the ficus, that are not stopped and, where these are concerned, it might be better to move them to cooler positions in the winter. However most of us, alas, cannot afford these high temperatures and it is more a question of keeping the room warm enough for our plants and ourselves. In any natural climate the highest temperatures are around midday, but many sitting rooms are kept cold during the day, when people are out at work, warm in the evening, when everyone is at home, but cool off during the late evening and the early morning after people have gone to bed.

Such a contradiction of natural rhythm is sufficient to disturb any plant and it is easy to see that keeping plants in good condition in the winter is less simple in the house than in a greenhouse. If you have some system of regular central heating, the problem is comparatively simple, but for rooms with only sporadic warmth, the matter is less straightforward. However, there are house plants to suit all conditions. It is as well to know what the average

temperature of your room is during the winter, otherwise the problem can be resolved only by a system of trial and error, during which you might well lose the plants that you most prize. It is fairly safe to say that no plant will tolerate the conditions that are to be found on a mantelpiece above a coal fire. The atmosphere is far too dry and the alternations of cold and roasting heat are too much for all plants, except the toughest succulents. Even if the temperature is equable, plants that are put too near the window risk being chilled, or even frosted, when the weather is very cold and they should be moved further into the room during these periods.

Even when the temperature is satisfactory, the dry atmosphere that we like in our rooms is not beneficial to plants. This, however, can easily be overcome, by placing the pots in a larger container and filling this container with some moisture-retentive material. Peat is most frequently used, but moss or mica powder does equally well. Some people get perfectly satisfactory results with damp newspaper, which is topped with moss to look more elegant. By these means we can maintain a moist atmos-

**1 The attractive leaves of Fittonia argyroneura add colour throughout the indoor year.**
**2 A collection of house plants including Hedera canariensis, Ficus elastica, Sansevieria, Dieffenbachia, Begonia masoniana, Maranta and Peperomia.**

1

phere in the immediate surroundings of the plant without either affecting the atmosphere of our rooms or the correct state of moisture of the soil ball. With this we come to the most crucial matter in the successful cultivation of house plants.

## Watering

Over-watering is a great threat to plants. Like human beings, they cannot live without water, but, again like human beings, they can be drowned. However, this analogy cannot be pressed too far. Human beings need water at regular intervals, but plants need water most when they are making growth. This is usually during the spring and summer. There is a correlation between the growth of the aerial portion of the plant, the portion we can see, and the growth of the roots which we can't see. If the plant is making new leaves and stems, we can be fairly sure that it is also making new roots. Unfortunately, the root growth is liable to precede the production of new leaves and so these latter may be prevented from developing if the soil is too dry at the appropriate period. On the other hand, if the soil is too wet, the roots cannot breathe and, far from developing, are liable to rot and, unless this process can be stopped immediately, the plant itself will succumb. We can guard against this to some extent by purely physical means. If we have an open soil mixture that drains rapidly and well, the risk of the soil becoming sodden and sour is reduced, although not, of course, obviated altogether. When to give water is only satisfactorily learned by experience, but the following hard and fast rules are generally acceptable.

1 When water is applied, it should be in sufficient quantity to moisten the whole of the soil ball. The water should be at room temperature. Rain water is preferable but not essential.

2 The soil should be allowed to dry out between waterings. This is not too easy to interpret. We do not want the soil to become dust dry, but on the other hand, we want to avoid saturation. A useful rule of thumb with clay pots and soil mixtures, is to strike the side of the pot with your knuckle. If the resultant sound is dull, watering is not needed, but if it is a ringing sound, water should be applied. With peat mixtures the weight of the pot is a more reliable indication. If it feels light, water is wanted, but not if it feels heavy. The same applies, but to a lesser extent, with soil mixtures in plastic pots. These are much the most difficult to gauge.

3 During cold weather plants make little or no growth and so require little water. Growth is also slowed down when there is little light. It is safe, therefore, during

**Hedera helix 'Chicago' and Spider Plant.**

the winter to keep all watering down to a minimum, even though the room may be kept at quite a high temperature. Naturally plants in warm rooms will require more than those in cool surroundings.

4 From about mid-April it is probable that growth will start and so more water may be required. Be cautious, nevertheless, until you see new leaves appearing. It is possible to knock the plant out of its pot to see if new roots (characterised by their white tips) are forming and to replace the soil ball without disturbance. When growth is vigorous water will be needed more frequently. 'Stopping' checks growth temporarily and watering should be on a reduced scale until a resumption of growth is seen.

5 By the end of August it is advisable to discourage much further growth and encourage the plant to ripen its new growth. This is done by keeping the plant as dry as possible.

6 The type of leaf will give some indication of the plant's requirements. Plants with thick leaves or with succulent leaves (such as the large-leaved ficus and sansevieria) can tolerate longer periods without water than thin-leaved plants. These latter will probably wilt when they become too dry and they should be watered at once. The thicker leaved plants will not wilt and so should be inspected frequently. Drought, unless acute, will not kill them but may cause subsequent leaf drop.

If leaves turn yellow and fall off, it usually indicates over-watering. However some plants, such as *Ficus benjamina,* will naturally shed their year-old leaves in the autumn and most plants shed a few leaves in the course of the year. Excessive defoliation is almost certainly due to incorrect watering; although it can be caused by under-watering as well as by over watering. If the plant becomes unsteady in the pot, this is generally due to root-rot caused by excessive water and is very difficult to arrest. Some leaves will wilt in the summer if they are in direct hot sunlight. If the soil appears to be satisfactorily moist, a syringeing of the leaves with water will generally restore them to their normal turgidity, and in any case, they will resume their normal appearance as soon as the sunlight goes.

Once the question of watering has been mastered, there are few other problems. Rooms are very dusty which spoils the appearance of the leaves of house plants and also prevents them from functioning properly. It is advisable, therefore, to clean the leaves every two or four weeks. This is best done with cotton wool and tepid water and the leaves should be sponged on both sides. New leaves are soft and easily damaged and should be left until they are older. Some people use milk, or oil, or flat beer to give the leaves a more glossy appearance, but these mixtures do not do the

**1 Maranta mackoyana must be protected from sunlight to keep its leaf colour.**
**2 A collection of Ferns in a bark container, with Helxine added in the front.**

leaves any good.

During the summer, when growth is most vigorous, the plants may be fed. A liquid feed is most easily applied and should be given according to the instructions on the bottle. Little and often is invariably better than doses in excess of those recommended. Unless the plant is really well-rooted, feeding should not be applied and is not necessary for plants that have been repotted. Repot-

ting is done in the early summer. For the majority of house plants the John Innes potting compost No 2 is the best. Plants are usually potted on into a pot one size larger. Plants from 5-inch pots are put into 6-inch pots and so on. The only exception is that the 4-inch pot is very rarely used and plants are moved from 3-inch to 5-inch pots. Plants with very thin roots such as begonias and peperomias do better in a mixture of 2 parts of leafmould to 1 part of sharp sand, while epiphytes, such as the bromeliads, are usually given a mixture of peat, leafmould and sharp sand. However, it is only rarely that epiphytes require any potting on, as they use the soil as an anchorage only. After being potted on the plants should be kept on the dry side until the roots have penetrated the new soil. It is best to move plants from 2-inch pots to 5-inch pots after a year, as the 3-inch pots dry out so quickly, but after that most house plants will need repotting only every other year. The second year the plant will need feeding.

The epiphytic bromeliads (aechmea, neoregelia, nidularium, guzmania, tillandsia and vriesia) need rather different treatment from most house plants. They have a rosette of strap-shaped leaves which form the so-called 'vase'. This must be kept full of water, preferably rain water. The mixture in which they are potted may be kept moist, but this is of minor importance, as the roots serve little purpose except anchorage and it is from the leaves that nutriment is absorbed. During the summer the merest trace of liquid feed may be added to the water in the vase, but this must be done with great discretion.

Most house plants are easily propagated if you have a greenhouse, although some, such as the large-leaved ficus, cordylines and dracaenas, need a good deal of heat to get them to root. There are a few that can easily be propagated in the home. The various tradescantias and zebrinas will root easily in water and so will *Cissus antarctica* and *Rhoicissus rhomboidea*. Shoots of succulents, such as *Sedum sieboldii* and aichryson will root easily, either in ordinary soil or in a mixture of equal parts of peat and sharp sand, which is an ideal mixture for most cuttings. Shoots of the various ivies, taken when they are half ripe, that is neither too young nor too woody, will root easily although rather slowly. The peperomias, with single leaves rising from the base, can be rooted from leaf stem cuttings. The leaf with its stem is pulled off and inserted in the peat and sand mixture, when a new

**1 The shining bright Umbrella Tree.**
**2 The flamboyant Poinsettia.**

plant will form at the base of the leaf stalk. Sansevierias will produce new leaves on rhizomes, but they do not root until a year has elapsed and should not, therefore, be severed from the main plant before this time. If, however, you can find the new rhizome without disturbing the plant and cut half-way through it, it will hasten the formation of roots at the base of the new leaf. Many of the climbing aroids produce aerial roots and these can be induced to develop in soil. These climbing aroids (philodendron, syngonium and scindapsus), will grow more luxuriantly if they are given a cylinder of wire stuffed with moss up which they can grow. However, the moss must be kept damp and this is not easy in the home. They can also be trained on blocks of cork bark.

### Keeping Pests at Bay

With good hygiene, you should have little trouble with house plant pests. The most troublesome is liable to be red spider

mite. This is a tiny mite which congregates in large numbers on the undersides of leaves, causing discoloration. The mites are not easy to see with the naked eye, but affected plants have a characteristic rough feel: This pest is usually associated with very dry conditions and these are liable to occur in rooms during the summer. If the leaves are regularly sponged, it is improbable that any serious infestation will occur. If it does, it is necessary to immerse the plant in water containing a suitable acaricide or in a white oil emulsion. Aphids may be found occasionally, clustering around the growing points, but aerosol sprays are available to control them. Some of the larger-leaved ficus may have scale insects on the underside of the leaves. If the plant is inspected regularly, there is little risk of this becoming serious. The scale insects may be removed with a matchstick.

A list of plants for rooms at specific heats follows below. For a far more detailed selection of the best plants for all sorts of conditions and how to cultivate them see the previous section of the book.

**Plants for unheated but frost-proof rooms**

*Aichryson × domesticum variegatum* This is a small variegated succulent, a hybrid of garden origin, with long, oval leaves, almost entirely ivory-white when young, later turning olive-green with an ivory margin.

*Aspidistra lurida* This, with its broad, dark green leaves, was once the most popular house plant of all, and it is once again returning to popularity, particularly the variegated forms.

*Billbergia nutans* A terrestrial bromeliad with bluebell-like flowers, but rather uninteresting leaves.

*Chlorophytum comosum* This is an attractive variegated plant, with long, narrow leaves, which forms new plants at the ends of the flower stems. It is sometimes called, inaccurately, *C. capense*.

*Cissus antarctica* A climbing plant that will grow anywhere except in very deep shade.

*Cordyline indivisa* and *Dracaena parrii* These are palm-like plants with many long narrow leaves. They should be given well-lit positions.

*Cyperus diffusus* The umbrella grass is very easy to grow, but rather dull on its own.

*× Fatshedera lizei* This is an intergeneric or bigeneric hybrid between *Fatsia* and *Hedera*. It makes a tall leggy plant, with

1 Peperomia magnoliaefolia needs far less water than most house plants.
2 Symbol of Victoriana, Aspidistra lurida, with long shining leaves.
3 Cyperus diffusus, the Umbrella Grass, an easily grown but uninteresting plant.
4 One of the small-leaved self-branching forms of Hedera canariensis, Indoor Ivy.
5 The Staghorn Fern, Platycerium bifurcatum.

1

2

3

4

dark green, five-lobed leaves. The variety *variegata*, has leaves with cream margins.

*Fatsia japonica* The castor oil plant. The variegated form is the most attractive.

*Hedera helix* There are numerous cultivars of the common ivy. Some are small-leaved, self-branching plants that do not require stopping, as they form sideshoots naturally. They like reasonably light situations and are slightly affected by gas fumes. The most popular cultivars are 'Chicago', 'Pittsburgh', *sagittaefolia*, 'Heisse' and 'Little Eva'. There are other cultivars that are not self-branching and need stopping two or three times in the spring and summer. The most popular are 'Glacier' and 'Golden Jubilee'. The latter, a most attractive plant, needs as bright a light as you can give it. The climbing, larger-leaved, cultivars, *marmorata* and *maculata aurea*, do not branch much, but any sickly winter growth should be removed in the spring. The forms of *Hedera canariensis, foliis variegatis* and 'Golden Leaf', do not break after stopping and can be grown in warmer situations than the forms of *H. helix*.

*Pittosporum eugenioides* This is a pleasant shrub with black stems and attractively shaped leaves. There is also a good variegated form.

*Rhoicissus rhomboidea* A vigorous vine-like plant with leaves composed of three leaflets. The best cultivar is 'Jubilee'.

*Saxifraga stolonifera* The well-known 'mother of thousands', with marbled leaves and flowers like those of 'London pride'. There is a variegated form, *tricolor,* which is attractive but difficult to keep in good condition. It probably requires more warmth.

*Sedum sieboldii variegatum* This has round, blue-green leaves with a yellow centre and heads of small pink flowers in the autumn. It is not truly evergreen and dies down each autumn, to reappear in February.

*Stenocarpus sinuatus* This is an attractive shrub with oak-like leaves, reddish when they first appear.

*Tradescantia fluviatilis* and *Zebrina pendula* Both these are known as the wandering Jew, and are very easy to grow and propagate. Only the variegated forms of the trandescantia are worth growing and any unvariegated growths should be removed immediately, when detected, otherwise the plant will revert to the ordinary green form.

**Plants for rooms with an average winter temperature of 50°F (10°C)**

*Begonia rex* and *most other Begonias* These like a somewhat shady position and are very susceptible to gas fumes. The pots should be plunged in moist peat to provide a humid atmosphere. The soil

1 The Canary Island Ivy, Hedera canariensis foliis variegatis.
2 A shining-leaved climber for a cool room, Rhoicissus rhomboidea.
3 Cissus antarctica, the Kangaroo Vine.
4 The young leaves of Stenocarpus sinuatus are reddish at first.
5 The Rubber Plant, Ficus elastica decora, lives happily in stuffy rooms.
6 The wavy-leaved form of the Indoor Fig is Ficus lyrata.
7 A variegated-leaved form of the Indoor Fig, Ficus schryveriana.
8 One of the Philodendrons that does not climb is P. bipinnatifidum.

5

6

7

8

should not be over-watered.

*Brassaia actinophylla (syn. Schefflera actino-phylla)* This is a vigorous shrub with glossy leaves, divided into five leaflets, eventually up to 1 foot across.

*Cissus sicyoides* This is a not very vigorous vine with palmate leaves on crimson leaf stalks. It dislikes gas fumes.

*Citrus mitis* The calamondin is a small orange with fragrant white flowers and small, rather tart, orange fruits. It is best stood outside in full sun during the summer. This ripens the wood and encourages the formation of flower buds, but turns the leaves a rather unhealthy colour. They will usually revert to a pleasant glossy green after being brought indoors again at the beginning of September.

*Ficus benjamina* An attractive small tree with a slightly pendulous habit, this sheds, each autumn, a quantity of leaves, but as it has previously produced plenty of foliage the plant is always pleasant to look at.

*Ficus elastica* There are many forms of the India-rubber tree available; the best unvariegated form is *decora*. The variegated forms (*doescheri, schryveriana, tricolor*) need more light.

*Monstera pertusa* This is usually called *M. deliciosa borsigiana;* it is similar in habit to the climbing philodendrons, but has large leaves that are perforated with

circular holes and the margins may be fringed. It needs a good deal of light, as, if it is too heavily shaded, the leaves will not develop the characteristic attractive perforations.

*Peperomia magnoliaefolia, P. obtusifolia,* and *P. glabella* The peperomias have a very small root system and very rarely require potting on. They will grow in shady situations and need far less water than most house plants.

*Philodendron bipinnatifidum* This is not one of the climbing philodendrons; it has very large, much divided leaves. Each leaf may be up to 2 feet long and 1½ feet across.

*Philodendron scandens, P. erubescens 'Burgundy', P. elegans* Climbing plants of the arum family, these have aerial roots rising from the stem at the base of each leaf-stalk. They will grow best if given cylinders of moss on which they can climb, but are satisfactory without this.

*Platycerium bifurcatum* The elk's horn or stag's horn fern, does well fastened to a block of cork wood. If this is done the plant must be immersed in a bucket of water from time to time, as ordinary watering is ineffective. The plant will grow in a pot, but is less effective when grown in this way.

*Sansevieria trifasciata laurentii* This has tall mottled leaves with cream margins and is a popular house plant. It should be kept quite dry during the winter, and watered moderately only at other times.

*Scindapsus aureus* This resembles a climbing *Philodendron,* but has golden variegated leaves. It needs ample light.

*Syngonium* Another climbing aroid, with leaves shaped like a goose's foot, this is a less vigorous climber than the philodendrons.

*Tetrastigma voinerianum* A very vigorous vine with leaves composed of five leaflets, that may be 10 inches across, this plant needs good light and plenty of room, as it may grow very tall.

**Plants for rooms with winter temperature 55—60°F (13—16°C)**

There are many more philodendrons, both terrestrial and climbing. The most attractive is *P. melanochryson.* This has heart-shaped, dark velvety-green leaves, purple-pink on the undersides. It is the juvenile form of the large-leaved *P. andreanum.*

*Anthurium scherzerianum* This has bright scarlet, waxy, 'painter's palette' flowers. It needs to be grown in a mixture of sphagnum moss and leafmould, which is aerated by broken crocks. It likes a moist atmosphere and must not be allowed to dry out.

*Aphelandra squarrosa* This is a handsome and popular plant with lance-shaped

1 The Rugby Football Plant, or Water Melon Plant, Peperomia sandersii.
2 The arrow-shaped leaves of Philodendron hastatum need frequent cleaning.
3 One of the climbing forms of Philodendron, P. scandens.
4 A young plant of the Mexican Breadfruit Plant, Monstera delicosa borsigiana. It is also sometimes called the Swiss Cheese Plant.
5 A young plant of Tetrastigma voineriana.
6 Sansevieria trifasciata laurentii, and Hedera 'Heiss' in the foreground.
7 The deeply cut leaves of Philodendron elegans are an attractive addition to any collection of indoor plants.
8 Scindapsus aureus, the Devil's Ivy.
9 Sansevieria trifasciata laurentii, or Mother-in-law's Tongue.

5

6

7

8

9

dark green leaves, with prominent ivory veins and pyramids of yellow flowers. The best cultivars are 'Brockfeld' and 'Silver Beauty'. The variety *louisae* is the one that is most generally grown.

*Bromeliads* Although the various bromeliads are more tolerant of cold than their exotic appearance would suggest, they will do best in this section. They will, however, survive at lower temperatures.

*Codiaeum variegatum* The 'crotons' have spectacularly coloured leaves in a multitude of different shapes and colours. They will not tolerate draughts, which cause leaf-drop and they need a well-lit position. They should not be stopped until they become too leggy, which means that no stopping should be done for two or three years, and then it is a question of cutting-back, rather than stopping. The sap of the plants is milky and flows freely, so, when plants are cut back, it is useful to have some cotton-wool handy to clean them up.

*Cordyline terminalis* These are the broad-leaved 'dracaenas' with colours of crimson and red in the young leaves. They are spectacular and not difficult to grow, except that they are liable to be infected by red spider mites.

*Dieffenbachia amoena* The dumb-canes have large, oblong-oval leaves, marbled with cream or yellow. The plants are spectacular, but very poisonous, and they are not recommended where there are children.

1

2

3

4

5

*Dizygotheca elegantissima* (syn. *Aralia elegantissima*) This plant has palmate, spidery leaves when young, although in mature specimens the leaves are considerably broader. Again red spider mites are the enemy.

*Dracaena fragrans, D. deremensis, D. goldieana* These are very beautiful shrubs with broad leaves, striped with various shades of silver, cream and yellow. The first named has the broadest leaves. They should never be stopped.

*Ficus lyrata* and *F. nekbudu* These are both handsome, large-leaved ficus. The leaves of the first are shaped like the body of a violin, the second has large, oblong-oval leaves with prominent cream veins. They should be examined frequently for

infestation by scale insects. These are usually on the underside of the leaves and may be removed with a match-stick. Neither plant should be over-watered in winter.

*Maranta* and *Calathea* These are plants with remarkably attractive leaves, that must be shielded from direct sunlight. They require a moister atmosphere than most houses can provide and the pots in which they are grown should, therefore, be put in bowls of moist peat or something similar.

*Peperomia argyreia, P. caperata, P. hederaefolia* Peperomias have single leaves rising from a common rootstock. *P. argyreia* (*P. sandersi*) is the most handsome with its rugby-football-shaped leaves of cream

1 A poisonous plant Dieffenbachia amoena, justifiably called Dumb Cane.
2 Dracaena massangeana, a spreading plant with variegated leaves.
3 Dracaena godseffiana has opposite leaves heavily spotted with cream and likes a warm room with plenty of light.
4 The Striped Dracaena produces whorls of green leaves, edged and heavily marked with cream.
5 In older plants of Dracaena marginata, the leaves are edged and veined red.

and grey. All these peperomias should be kept fairly dry, but given a moist atmosphere surrounding them.

*Spathiphyllum wallisii* This is grown for its attractive, white, arum-like flowers, which may appear in the autumn.

# Caring for Pot Plants

A very large number of flowering plants are raised each year in pots to be sold for the decoration of rooms, shops, etc. The quantity produced and the selection of genera and species to be grown are governed more by commercial than horticultural considerations. This means that many of the most delightful plants are not grown because they are either unsuitable for room decoration or are too expensive to produce. However, in keeping with the law of supply and demand, more of these plants are grown today.

There is now, for example, a very extensive Christmas trade in poinsettias; plants which not so many years ago were the prerogative of those gardeners who had the advantage of a heated greenhouse. The poinsettia is an example of the fluctuations in popularity due to the qualities that growers require in a pot plant that is destined for room decoration. As originally introduced the poinsettia was a rather tall plant, which showed great susceptibility to draughts. The Edwardians would put them in their jardinières, but a few days after being brought into the house all the leaves would fall off leaving a straight, bare stem except for the rosette of scarlet bracts at the top.

As the plants have such brilliant flowers at the darkest time of the winter efforts were made to obtain shorter plants which could be used for table decoration. For this purpose cuttings were taken rather late in the season and the plants put on shelves in the greenhouse, suspended near the glass. In the days when people of even moderate means could afford gardeners, a man could be running up and down ladders half the day to water the plants that were often placed 10 feet from the ground. Nurserymen would also grow these rather expensively produced plants, and they cultivated comparatively dwarf plants. The plants still showed susceptibility to draughts and they would often be put into rooms that might be roasting hot at night, but barely frost-proof during the day-time. Heating generally came from an open, coal fire and this would often only be lit in the evening or afternoon. Under these conditions the poinsettia was not really a very popular commercial plant.

As the twentieth century advanced the use of central heating became more widespread, particularly in North America, where the winters are so cold that open fire heating was quite inadequate. The atmosphere produced by central heating is more congenial to tropical plants, such as the poinsettia. On the other hand labour and heating both became more expensive and it was no longer commercially practical to produce dwarf plants in the old way.

The poinsettia was sold as a rather tall, lanky plant.

At the same time a certain amount of selection was going on to find a plant that would be less susceptible to draughts and to violent fluctuations of temperature. Even if the room were draught-proof, the plant had been brought from the nursery to the shop and from the shop to the purchaser's home, and this would defoliate the poinsettia through a succession of chills and heat. There was some success in this selection to find a plant which would resist draughts, and before the Second World War there were strains of poinsettia which were fairly retentive of their leaves.

The next step came after the war with the discovery of chemicals that would dwarf a plant by simple application. It was this that really transformed the situation and enhanced the commercial possibilities of the poinsettia. It became possible to produce a compact scarlet-flowered plant for Christmas blooming. The selection of the 'Mikkelsen' strain, which will retain its leaves under the most adverse conditions, has resulted in a plant that has almost all the qualities that the grower and purchaser of pot plants requires. It is a plant that is colourful at a time when there is little colour outside, sufficiently compact to be placed on tables without appearing too intrusive, and will maintain itself in good condition without too much attention.

In describing the qualities that the breeders of the poinsettia tried to obtain the desirable features of the pot plant have been shown. It is chiefly in the months between October and April that pot plants are most in demand. They should be fairly easy to manage, which means that they do not require great heat or a very wet atmosphere. They should be compact, because shrubs some 5 feet in height even though they are covered in flowers for two months on end would be far too large for most rooms. The plants should give a good display of blossom, because a plant that has a long-flowering season, but never bears more than a few flowers at a time, will not be very popular commercially. That is one of the reasons why the gardenia has never become very popular as a pot plant; it has a long flowering season, but seldom a very large display of blossom. This might be overcome, in view of the plant's fragrance, if it were slightly more easy to manage.

People will grow difficult plants such as cyclamen and saintpaulias provided the display is sufficiently rewarding, and they will grow easy plants that are less colourful, but they will not take trouble over plants that are neither easy nor very brilliant. Possibly, if there were a demand for a slow-growing, rather difficult plant, such as *Medinilla mag-nifica*, growers would develop a strain that was comparatively easy to propagate rapidly.

**Plants indoors** Keeping a plant in good condition in a living-room is more difficult than doing so in a greenhouse. It is usually easy enough to provide suitable temperatures and there are plants to suit most conditions. The difficulties that are to be faced are more concerned with light and with atmospheric humidity. Plants in nature or in most greenhouses (lean-to's) are an exception, and receive light from all sides and from above. Plants in rooms are generally illuminated on one side only.

Plants in the wild, and in a well-managed greenhouse, grow in a humid atmosphere. The amount of humidity depends on either rainfall or on the way the greenhouse is damped down, but the atmosphere is moist. In rooms, particularly during the winter months, the air tends to be dry. Plants that grow in deserts appreciate dry conditions, but hot deserts generally have brilliant light; a combination that is not too easy to reproduce in the greenhouse, and well-nigh impossible in domestic rooms. The choice of room plants is therefore restricted to those that normally like rather shaded conditions and those that survive reasonably well in a rather dry atmosphere.

The problem of providing atmospheric humidity can be partly overcome by plunging the pot, or pots, into some other container, and filling the interstices with any absorbent material, such as peat, moss, vermiculite, sand, or even wet newspaper. This material is kept always moist, so that watered material will constantly surround the plant and contribute the necessary moisture to the air. This is fairly effective, but it is not the same as a uniformly humid atmosphere. In some rooms of the house, such as kitchens and bathrooms, the atmosphere is naturally rather steamy and many plants will thrive better in such situations. Nowadays, when the kitchen often serves as a dining room as well, there is much to be said for having plants in it, but there is usually a space problem in such rooms and this may prevent having your plants there. Although plunging the pots is only partially effective, it is sufficient to enable you to preserve a large number of flowering pot plants.

The problem of providing light can be partially overcome by turning the plant slightly each day, so that every part of the plant is illuminated in turn. Plants such as the Christmas and Easter cactus will resent this and drop their buds, but most flowering plants will appreciate all parts of the plant receiving light. Rooms with a bay window can have their plants placed so that they are illuminated from three sides, but the bay is sometimes rather cold and draughty.

Cool conditions will do no harm to flowering plants, provided that the cold is not excessive, but draughts are often killing, causing the buds to drop before opening and often resulting in defoliation. Plants placed on window sills usually receive sufficient light. However, unless the windows are double glazed the plants should be removed to the centre of the room when conditions are frosty.

Most of the winter-flowering pot plants that are sold are plants that are suitable for the house heated with coal fires, but which are not really suited to modern central heating. Plants such as the poinsettia and the African violet (saintpaulia) thrive on temperatures up to 70°F (21°C), but azaleas and greenhouse primulas will find such temperatures too high. As a result, they come rapidly into flower and soon drop all their blossoms. At a temperature of 55°F (13°C), an azalea will remain attractive for six or eight weeks; under warmer conditions it will last a far shorter time.

The warm centrally-heated rooms of modern buildings will encourage the introduction of plants like the poinsettia. In the USA the giant cyclamen is now unknown as a flowering pot plant for home decoration, as it will not survive at the high temperatures that are considered necessary in that country. It is considerably less popular in Britain

1 Begonia 'Cleopatra,' always a popular pot plant with its pink flowers.
2 The ever-popular Saintpaulia.

than it used to be. This may be not only because many people now keep their rooms at too high a temperature to suit these plants, it may also be because people have realised that it is extremely difficult to keep in good condition in the home.

Commercial growers found that it was necessary to devote a greenhouse entirely to the cultivation of cyclamen, and amateurs have found that they do not mix easily with other greenhouse plants, so that altogether they are not the best of plants for room decoration. Apart from this, they are showy and can be produced fairly cheaply and will, continue in flower over a long period in the right conditions. Given a temperature of around 55–60°F (13–16°C) and good lighting they can be kept going in rooms, but they are very liable to become drawn and floppy.

Watering, which is a problem with pot plants, is rather more critical with cyclamen. It is a truism to say that more plants are drowned than are lost any other way. Indeed there is now an opposite tendency and plants are sometimes kept too dry. Plants that are in flower or shortly to come into flower are thirsty plants and will usually take ample supplies of water. It is not a good idea to turn on the cold tap and use the water immediately. This water is generally far too cold and its application will lower the soil temperature and either check root growth or possibly kill the roots altogether.

Generally, the water should be at the same temperature as the atmosphere. To achieve this you can either store your water for 24 hours in the room in which your plants are, or, more simply, you can add some hot water to the cold to get the correct tepid temperature. If you have facilities for collecting rain water, which is much appreciated by the plants, then you will want to store it until it reaches room temperature. The frequency with which you water will depend on a large number of factors. There is more evaporation from clay pots than from the plastic ones, so that clay pots will require water more frequently. However, if the pots have been plunged in some absorbent medium, there will be less evaporation from clay pots. Many plants, among which begonias and fuchsias are more prone to this, are liable to drop their buds if either the soil or the atmosphere is too dry.

Excessive wetness can also cause bud-drop. When plants are watered, this should be done thoroughly. The whole of the space between the soil level and the rim of the pot should be filled with water, which should percolate through the soil and moisten it all throughout. If the water appears to run straight through and out at the end, it is a sign that the soil has become too dry. In this case place the pot in a bucket of water, the level of the water being above the rim of the pot, and leave it there until bubbles cease to rise to the surface. Then remove the pot and firm the soil around the edge of the pot with your thumbs. After that you should be able to resume normal watering.

Composts without soil and mixtures that are based mainly on peat, such as are used for azaleas and winter heathers, will dry out more rapidly than composts that contain a large quantity of loam. The fact that the surface of the soil appears dry does not necessarily indicate that the whole soil ball has dried out. However, when you see the surface looking dry it is usually safe to water the following day. Azaleas have a sort of tide mark on their trunk, which gives you an indication of their requirements. It should be about half an inch above the

**1** Azaleas of various kinds, apart from the so-called 'Indian Azaleas' sold by florists, make excellent, free-flowering pot plants. They will flower over a longer period if the temperature in the room is not too high.
**2** The silky 'tassels' of Celosia plumosa, the Prince of Wales's Feather, are long lasting.
**3** Begonias of the semperflorens type are available in various colours.

level of the soil. If it is higher, the plant has had too much water, if it is lower it requires watering. Flowering pot plants are best purchased when they still have plenty of well-developed flower buds. If the plant is in full flower it will not last for long, while if the buds are too immature, they may not recover from the shock of changing atmospheres. It is not unusual for cyclamen to be offered for sale with two or three flowers out and a number of barely-developed flower buds. It is very unlikely that these buds will develop under room conditions and such plants should be avoided.

The majority of pot plants that are offered commercially thrive best in a temperature ranging from 55–60 F (13–16 C) and cannot be expected to persist for so long with higher temperatures. One or two such as cyclamen and cinerarias may even dislike very high temperatures and collapse. Plants such as azaleas and greenhouse primulas will tolerate high temperatures, but will flower and fade at great speed. During the winter months all plants should be given as much light as possible.

The following is a list of the principal pot plants for room use arranged according to the months in which they will flower:

*January* Begonia 'Gloire de Lorraine'; *B. manicata; Rhododendron simsii (Azalea indica)*; cultivars, *Erica gracilis* and *hyemalis;* Poinsettia; Cyclamen. *February* Indian azaleas; Cyclamen; *Primula malacoides,* Hippeastrum. *March* Indian Azaleas; Cyclamen; *Primula malacoides* and *P. obconica;* Cineraria. *April* In addition to the March plants, schizanthus, calceolaria, *Primula sinensis;* and the Easter Cactus, *Rhipsalidopsis rosea. May* Schizanthus, Ealceolaria, forced hydrangea, regal pelargoniums, *Boronia megastigma. June* Regal pelargoniums, zonal pelargoniums, hydrangea, fuchsias, *Rochea coccinea. July* fuchsia, *Exacum affine,* Alonsoa, gloxinia, begonia; *Companula isophylla. August* As July with browallia, achimenes; torenia *September* As August, chrysanthemum. *October* chrysanthemum, gesneria, x Smithiantha, cyclamen. *November* Chrysanthemum, begonias, poinsettia, cyclamen, *Capsicum annuum. December* Poinsettia, Begonia 'Gloire de Lorraine', *Solanum capsicastrum,* azaleas, cyclamen, Christmas cactus, *Capsicum annuum, Erica gracilis* and *E. hyemalis.*

Saintpaulias can be purchased in flower in most months of the year.

**1 Schizanthus, the Poor Man's Orchid, is an annual which makes a decorative flowering pot plant. The leaves are much divided and fern-like and the flowers are in a wide range of colours. 2 Cyclamen persicum, the florist's Cyclamen, a winter-blooming plant which flowers in many colours including this attractive pink.**

# Repotting

There are several important stages in the cultivation of a plant and one of these is the planting of plants in pots. This is known as potting. The move is dictated by the vigour of the plant, especially its root system. Once it outgrows its original soil area in a pot, it is necessary to provide more room for the root development and the plant has to be moved on or potted into a larger pot. If the plant is being raised from seed or a cutting, it will be necessary to give it more root room eventually and the next move is into a small pot.

Although many plants will eventually be planted out into the ground, some will continue their growth and produce their foliage or flowering displays in pots. These must be large enough to provide adequate root room and feeding facilities. It will be appreciated, therefore, that the potting of plants is a progressive and logical sequence of events.

The time to pot plants must depend on what is being grown. Most of the general potting, however, takes place in the early part of each year—usually from February until late May.

Success with potting depends on the use of a suitable soil mixture. Fortunately one formula is all that is required as this contains all the essential ingredients in the correct proportions. This is the John Innes potting compost and it can be purchased, ready made up, from local garden shops or mixed as described in the article on Compost, under the subheading Soil composts.

Soilless composts are becoming increasingly popular with many gardeners. These are obtainable in various proprietary formulations.

Before potting begins it is important to make sure that all pots are thoroughly clean. Now that plastic pots have practically superseded clay ones, this is no problem. Drainage is important and clay pots will require small broken pieces of crock placed over the drainage holes, or special plastic mesh can be used for the plastic pots.

When the crocks are in place, a little coarse soil (the residue from the sieve is ideal) should be placed on top. This is followed by a small amount of the prepared John Innes potting compost or other mixture. To remove a pot plant for potting on into a pot of larger size, the pot and plant is turned upside down and the rim of the pot rapped smartly on the edge of the staging, bench or other suitable solid surface. If the fingers of one hand are kept over the soil and on either side of the plant's stem, the loosened soil bulk can be guided out of the pot.

The plant should then be placed on top of the soil in the new pot and more soil should be carefully trickled or poured in around the inside of the pot. Gentle firming is needed and this is done with the fingers, pressing evenly all round but a little way away from the plant's stem. A final sharp rap of the pot on the staging or bench will settle the soil even further, and any topping up with extra soil can be done afterwards. Make sure that the level of the soil is a little below the rim of the pot to allow for watering.

Where plants are being potted into pot sizes of 6 inches and over, much firmer potting is required. This can be achieved with a short piece of blunt-ended stick. It is used as a rammer (not *too* hard) to compress the soil between the inside edge of the pot and the plant's soil ball.

**Propagating fuchsias by 1 using lots of pots to ensure drainage 2 repotting to make sure the roots have plenty of room and 3 firming round the edge of the soil.**

Make sure that the potting soil is just moist. Under no circumstances should the mixture be dry when potting is started. It is a good plan to soak the soil several hours before it is required, and then to allow surplus moisture to drain away. If the potting compost is neither too wet nor too dry, a handful when picked up and squeezed firmly in the hand should retain its shape, but should then crumble when thrown back on the heap of prepared soil.

Once the plants have been potted, they should be given shady conditions to prevent drooping or flagging. Blinds or a little shading spray on the glass will help. Keep the plants watered regularly but apply sufficient only to keep the soil moist. As soon as the plants have established themselves and overcome the slight check to growth which is inevitable with potting, they can be placed in full light.

# Index